T0002375

THIS IS *IT*

THIS IS
IT

AND OTHER ESSAYS
ON ZEN AND
SPIRITUAL EXPERIENCE

—

Alan Watts

VINTAGE BOOKS
A DIVISION OF RANDOM HOUSE
NEW YORK

COVER PHOTO: ERNST HAAS

First Vintage Books Edition, April 1973

Copyright © 1958, 1960 by Alan W. Watts

Library of Congress Cataloging in Publication Data

Watts, Alan Wilson, 1915-
  This is it.

  Reprint of the 1960 ed.
  1. Mysticism 2. Zen Buddhism. I. Title.
[BL625.W35 1973] 294.3 4   72-8394
ISBN 0-394-71904-2

49 48 47 46 45 44 43

Printed in the United States of America

TO ANN
daughter and dancer,
with love

CONTENTS

PREFACE

Although written at different times during the past four years, the essays here gathered together have a common point of focus—the spiritual or mystical experience and its relation to ordinary material life. Having said this, I am instantly aware that I have used the wrong words; and yet there are no satisfactory alternatives. Spiritual and mystical suggest something rarefied, otherworldly, and loftily religious, opposed to an ordinary material life which is simply practical and commonplace. The whole point of these essays is to show the fallacy of·this opposition, to show that the spiritual is not to be separated from the material, nor the wonderful from the ordinary. We need, above all, to disentangle ourselves from habits of speech and thought which set the two apart, making it impossible for us to see that *this*—the immediate, everyday, and present experience—is IT, the entire and ultimate point for the existence of a universe. But the recognition that the two are one comes to pass in an elusive, though relatively common, state of consciousness which has fascinated me beyond all else since I was seventeen years old.

I am neither a preacher nor a reformer, for I like to write and talk about this way of seeing things as one sings in the bathtub or splashes in the sea. There is no mission, nor intent to convert, and yet I believe that if this state of consciousness could become more universal, the pretentious nonsense which passes for the serious business of the world would dissolve in laughter. We should see at once that the high ideals for which we are killing and regimenting each other are empty and abstract substitutes for the unheeded miracles that surround us—not only in the obvious wonders of nature but also in the overwhelmingly uncanny fact of mere existence. Not for one moment do I believe that such an awakening would deprive us of energy or social concern. On the contrary, half the delight of it—though infinity has no halves—is to share it with others, and because the spiritual and the material are inseparable this means the sharing of life and things as well as insight. But the possibility of this depends entirely upon the presence of the vision which could transform us into the kind of people who can do it, not upon exhortation or appeals to our persistent, but consistently uncreative, sense of guilt. Yet it would spoil it all if we felt obliged, by that same sense, to have the vision.

For, contradictory as it may sound, it seems to me that the deepest spiritual experience can arise only in moments of a selfishness so complete that it transcends itself, by "the way down and out," which is perhaps why Jesus found the companionship of publicans and sinners preferable to that of the righteous and respectable. It is a sort of first step to accept one's own selfishness without the deception of trying to wish it were otherwise, for a man who is not all of one piece is perpetually paralyzed by trying to go in two directions at once. As a Turkish proverb puts it, "He who sleeps on the floor will not fall out of bed." And so, when the sinner realizes that even his repentance is sinful, he may perhaps for the first time "come to himself" and be whole. Spiritual awakening is the difficult process whereby the increasing realization that everything is as wrong as it can be flips suddenly into the realization that everything is as right as it can be. Or better, everything is as It as it can be.

Only two of the essays that follow have been published previously, "Zen and the Problem of Control" and "Beat Zen, Square Zen, and Zen," the former in the first issue of *Contact* and the latter in *The Chicago Review* for the summer of 1958, and then, in expanded form, as a separate booklet by City Lights Books of San Francisco. I wish to thank the respective editors and publishers concerned for permission to include them in this volume.

Because of the rather personal and, indirectly, auto-biographical nature of most of these essays, it seemed appropriate to include here a bibliography of the books and major articles which I have written to date.

San Francisco, 1960   ALAN W. WATTS

I

THIS IS *IT*

THE most impressive fact in man's spiritual, intellectual, and poetic experience has always been, for me, the universal prevalence of those astonishing moments of insight which Richard Bucke called "cosmic consciousness." There is no really satisfactory name for this type of experience. To call it mystical is to confuse it with visions of another world, or of gods and angels. To call it spiritual or metaphysical is to suggest that it is not also extremely concrete and physical, while the term "cosmic consciousness" itself has the unpoetic flavor of occultist jargon. But from all historical times and cultures we have reports of this same unmistakable sensation emerging, as a rule, quite suddenly and unexpectedly and from no clearly understood cause.

To the individual thus enlightened it appears as a vivid and overwhelming certainty that the universe, precisely as it is at this moment, as a whole and in every one of its parts, is so completely *right* as to need no explanation or justification beyond what it simply is. Existence not only ceases to be a problem; the mind is so wonder-struck at the self-evident and self-sufficient fitness of things as they are, including what would ordinarily be thought the very worst, that it cannot find any word strong enough to express the perfection and beauty of the experience. Its clarity sometimes gives the sensation that the world has become transparent or luminous, and its simplicity the sensation that it is pervaded and ordered by a supreme intelligence. At the same time it is usual for the individual to feel that the whole world has become his own body, and that whatever he is has not only become, but always has been, what everything else is. It is not that he loses his identity to the point of feeling that he actually looks out through all other eyes, becoming literally omniscient, but rather that his individual consciousness and existence is a point of view temporarily adopted by something immeasurably greater than himself.

The central core of the experience seems to be the conviction, or insight, that the immediate *now*, whatever its nature, is the goal and fulfillment of all living. Surrounding and flowing from this insight is an emotional ecstasy, a sense of intense relief, freedom, and lightness, and often of almost unbearable love for the world, which is, however, secondary. Often, the pleasure of the experience is confused with the experience and the insight lost in the ecstasy, so that in trying to retain the secondary effects of the experience the individual misses its point—that the immediate *now* is complete even when it is not ecstatic. For ecstasy is a necessarily impermanent contrast in the constant fluctuation of our feelings. But insight, when clear enough, persists; having once understood a particular skill, the facility tends to remain.

The terms in which a man interprets this experience are naturally drawn from the religious and philosophical ideas of his culture, and their differences often conceal its basic identity. As water seeks the course of least resistance, so the emotions clothe themselves in the symbols that lie most readily to hand, and the association is so swift and automatic that the symbol may appear to be the very heart of the experience. Clarity —the disappearance of problems—suggests light, and in moments of such acute clarity there may be the physical sensation of light penetrating everything. To a theist this will naturally seem to be a glimpse of the presence of God, as in the celebrated testimony of Pascal:

> The year of grace 1654,
> Monday the 23rd of November, St. Clement's day. • • •
> From about half past ten in the evening
> until about half past twelve, midnight,
>> FIRE
> God of Abraham. God of Isaac. God of Jacob
>> not of the philosophers and the wise.
> Certainty, joy, certainty, feeling, joy, peace.

Or in a case quoted by William James:

The very heavens seemed to open and pour down rays of light and glory. Not for a moment only, but all day and night, floods of light and glory seemed to pour through my soul, and oh, how I was changed, and everything became new. My horses and hogs and everybody seemed changed.

But clarity may also suggest transparency, or the sense that the world confronting us is no longer an obstacle and the body no longer a burden, and to a Buddhist this will just as naturally call to mind the doctrine of reality as the ungraspable, indefinable Void (*sunyata*).

I came back into the hall and was about to go to my seat when the whole outlook changed. A broad expanse opened, and the ground appeared as if all caved in. . . . As I looked around and up and down, the whole universe with its multitudinous sense-objects now appeared quite different; what was loathsome before, together with ignorance and passions, was now seen to be nothing else but the outflow of my own inmost nature which in itself remained bright, true, and transparent.[1]

As one and the same pain may be described either as a hot pang or as a cold sting, so the descriptions of this experience may take forms that seem to be completely opposed. One person may say that he has found the answer to the whole mystery of life, but somehow cannot put it into words. Another will say that there

[1] Yüan-chou (*d.* 1287), quoted by Suzuki, *Essays in Zen Buddhism,* vol. 2, p. 92.

never was a mystery and thus no answer to it, for what the experience made clear to him was the irrelevance and artificiality of all our questions. One declares himself convinced that there is no death, his true self being as eternal as the universe. Another states that death has simply ceased to matter, because the present moment is so complete that it requires no future. One feels himself taken up and united with a life infinitely other than his own. But as the beating of the heart may be regarded as something that *happens* to you or something that you *do*, depending on the point of view, so another will feel that he has experienced, not a transcendent God, but his own inmost nature. One will get the sense that his ego or self has expanded to become the entire universe, whereas another will feel that he has lost himself altogether and that what he called his ego was never anything but an abstraction. One will describe himself as infinitely enriched, while another will speak of being brought to such absolute poverty that he owns not even his mind and body, and has not a care in the world.

Rarely is the experience described without metaphors that might be misleading if taken literally. But in reading Bernard Berenson's *Sketch for a Self-Portrait* I came across a passage which is one of the simplest and "cleanest" accounts of it I have ever seen.

It was a morning in early summer. A silver haze shimmered and trembled over the lime trees. The air was laden with their fragrance. The temperature was like a caress. I remember—I need not recall—that I climbed up a tree stump and felt suddenly immersed in Itness. I did not call it by that name. I had no need for words. It and I were one.[2]

Just "It"—as when we use the word to denote the superlative, or the exact point, or intense reality, or what we were always looking for. Not the neuter sense of the mere object, but something still more alive and far wider than the personal, and for which we use this simplest of words because we have no word for it.

It is especially difficult to find the right means of expression for the experience in the cultural context of Christianity. For while this enlightenment comes just as much to Christians as to anyone else, the Christian mystic has always been in danger of conflict with the defenders of orthodoxy. Christian dogmatics insist firmly upon the radical difference between God and his created universe, as between God and the human soul. They insist upon God's eternal opposition to and abhorrence of evil and sin, and, since these are very present realities, upon the effective salvation of the world only at the end of time. Even then, hell will remain forever as the state of permanent imprisonment and torment for the forces of evil. Nevertheless, the doctrine of omnipotence—that nothing, not even sin, can happen without the permission of God's will—makes it possible even in this difficult framework for the Christian

[2] Bernard Berenson, *Sketch for a Self-Portrait*, p. 18. Pantheon Books, New York, 1949.

mystic to express the unspeakable doctrine that "sin is behovable, but all shall be well, and all shall be well, and all manner of thing shall be well." [3]

The Christian sense of the reality of evil and of time and history as the process of overcoming evil remains with us so strongly even in the post-Christian intellectual climate of today that we have difficulty in accepting the "cosmic consciousness" as more than an inspiring hallucination. Admissible it may be as the vision of some "far-off divine event" in the future, but with our progressive view of the world it seems impossible to accept it as a vision of the way things *are*. Even in the description which Bucke gives of his own experience there is a significant use of the future tense:

> All at once, without warning of any kind, I found myself wrapped in a flame-colored cloud. For an instant I thought of fire, an immense conflagration somewhere close by in that great city; the next, I knew that the fire was within myself. Directly afterward there came upon me a sense of exultation, of immense joyousness accompanied or immediately followed by an intellectual illumination impossible to describe. Among other things, I did not merely come to believe, but I saw that the universe is not composed of dead matter, but is, on the contrary, a

[3] Dame Julian of Norwich (1342—c. 1414), *Revelations of Divine Love*, xxvii. Ed. Grace Warrack. London, 1949. "Behovable" has the sense of "playing a necessary part." Compare the celebrated passage in the Roman liturgy of Holy Saturday, "O truly necessary sin of Adam, which the death of Christ has blotted out! O happy fault, that merited such and so great a redeemer!"

living Presence; I became conscious in myself of eternal life. It was not a conviction that I would have eternal life, but a consciousness that I possessed eternal life then; I saw that all men are immortal; that the cosmic order is such that without any peradventure all things work together for the good of each and all; that the foundation principle of the world, of all the worlds, is what we call love, and that the happiness of each and all is *in the long run* absolutely certain. The vision lasted a few seconds and was gone; but the memory of it and the sense of the reality of what it taught has remained during the quarter of a century which has since elapsed.[4]

Nevertheless, the "consciousness that I possessed eternal life *then*" corresponds to the Buddhist realization that "all things are in Nirvana from the very beginning," and that the enlightenment or awakening is not the creation of a new state of affairs but the recognition of what always *is*.

Such experiences imply, then, that our normal perception and valuation of the world is a subjective but collective nightmare. They suggest that our ordinary sense of practical reality—of the world as seen on Monday morning—is a construct of socialized conditioning and repression, a system of selective inattention whereby we are taught to screen out aspects and rela-

[4] Quoted from a privately printed account of the experience by William James, *Varieties of Religious Experience*, p. 399. London, 1929. Italics mine.

tions within nature which do not accord with the rules of the game of civilized life. Yet the vision almost invariably includes the realization that this very restriction of consciousness is also part of the eternal fitness of things. In the words of the Zen master Gensha:

> If you understand, things are such as they are;
> If you do not understand, things are such as they are—

this "such as they are" being the utterly unproblematic and self-sufficient character of this eternal now in which, as Chuang-tzu said,

> A duck's legs, though short, cannot be lengthened without discomfort to the duck; a crane's legs, though long, cannot be shortened without discomfort to the crane.

For in some way the vision seems to come about through accepting the rightness of the fact that one does not have it, through being willing to be as imperfect as one is—perfectly imperfect.

Now it is easy to see how this way of seeing things might be acceptable in cultures without the sense of hope and history, how, indeed, it might be the only basis for a philosophy that would make life tolerable. Indeed, it is very probable that the "historical dynamism" of the Christian West is a rather recent theological discovery, for we can no longer sing, without qualms of the social conscience, the *laissez-faire* hymn which says:

The rich man in his castle, the poor man at his gate,
He made them high or lowly, and ordered their estate—

and then go on to exclaim:

All things bright and beautiful, all creatures great and small,
All things wise and wonderful, the Lord God made them all!

But, even though it may be exploited for this purpose,
the experience itself is in no sense a philosophy designed to justify or to desensitize oneself to the in-
equalities of life. Like falling in love, it has a minimal
connection with any particular cultural background or
economic position. It descends upon the rich and the
poor, the moral and the immoral, the happy and the
miserable without distinction. It carries with it the overwhelming conviction that the world is in every respect
a miracle of glory, and though this might logically
exclude the necessity to share the vision with others
and awaken them from their nightmare the usual reaction is a sense, not of duty, but of sheer delight in
communicating the experience by word or deed.

From this new perspective the crimes and follies of
man's ordinary nightmare life seem neither evil nor
stupid but simply pitiable. One has the extraordinarily
odd sensation of seeing people in their mean or mali-
cious pursuits looking, at the same time, like gods—as
if they were supremely happy without knowing it.
As Kirillov puts it in Dostoyevsky's *The Possessed,*

"Man is unhappy because he doesn't know he's happy.
It's only that. That's all, that's all! If anyone finds out he'll
become happy at once, that minute. . . . It's all good. I
discovered it all of a sudden."

"And if anyone dies of hunger," [asks Stavrogin], "and
if anyone insults and outrages the little girl, is that good?"

"Yes! And if anyone blows his brains out for the baby,
that's good too. And if anyone doesn't, that's good too.
It's all good, all. It's good for all those who know that it's
all good. If they knew that it was good for them, it would
be good for them, but as long as they don't know it's good
for them, it will be bad for them. That's the whole idea,
the whole of it! . . . They're bad because they don't
know they're good. When they find out, they won't out-
rage a little girl. They'll find out that they're good and
they'll all become good, every one of them." [5]

Ordinarily one might feel that there is a shocking contrast between the marvellous structure of the human
organism and its brain, on the one hand, and the uses
to which most people put it, on the other. Yet there
could perhaps be a point of view from which the natural
wonder of the organism simply outshines the degrading
performances of its superficial consciousness. In a
somewhat similar way this strange opening of vision
does not permit attention to remain focussed narrowly

[5] Dostoyevsky, *The Possessed*, pp. 240-41. Trans. Constance Garnett.
Modern Library, New York, 1936.

upon the details of evil; they become subordinate to the all-pervading intelligence and beauty of the total design.

Such insight has not the slightest connection with "shallow optimism" nor with grasping the meaning of the universe in terms of some neat philosophical simplification. Beside it, *all* philosophical opinions and disputations sound like somewhat sophisticated versions of children yelling back and forth—" 'Tis!" " 'Tisn't!" " 'Tis!" " 'Tisn't!"—until (if only the philosophers would do likewise) they catch the nonsense of it and roll over backwards with hoots of laughter. Furthermore, so far from being the smug rationalization of a Mr. Pangloss, the experience has a tendency to arise in situations of total extremity or despair, when the individual finds himself without any alternative but to surrender himself entirely.

Something of this kind came to me in a dream when I was about eight years old. I was sick at the time and almost delirious with fever, and in the dream I found myself attached face-downward and spread-eagled to an immense ball of steel which was spinning about the earth. I knew in this dream with complete certainty that I was doomed to be spun in this sickening and terrifying whirl forever and ever, and the conviction was so intense that there was nothing for it but to give up—for this was hell itself and nothing lay before me but a literal everlastingness of pain. But in the moment when I surrendered, the ball seemed to strike against a mountain and disintegrate, and the next thing I knew was that I was sitting on a stretch of warm sand with nothing left of the ball except crumpled fragments of sheet-metal scattered around me. This was not, of course, the experience of "cosmic consciousness," but simply of the fact that release in extremity lies through and not away from the problem.

That other experience came much later, twice with intensity, and other times with what might be called more of a glow than a brilliant flash. Shortly after I had first begun to study Indian and Chinese philosophy, I was sitting one night by the fire, trying to make out what was the right attitude of mind for meditation as it is practiced in Hindu and Buddhist disciplines. It seemed to me that several attitudes were possible, but as they appeared mutually exclusive and contradictory I was trying to fit them into one—all to no purpose. Finally, in sheer disgust, I decided to reject them all and to have no special attitude of mind whatsoever. In the force of throwing them away it seemed that I threw myself away as well, for quite suddenly the weight of my own body disappeared. I felt that I owned nothing, not even a self, and that nothing owned me. The whole world became as transparent and un-obstructed as my own mind; the "problem of life" simply ceased to exist, and for about eighteen hours I and everything around me felt like the wind blowing leaves across a field on an autumn day.

The second time, a few years later, came after a

period when I had been attempting to practice what Buddhists call "recollection" (*smriti*) or constant awareness of the immediate present, as distinct from the usual distracted rambling of reminiscence and anticipation. But, in discussing it one evening, someone said to me, "But why *try* to live in the present? Surely we are always completely *in* the present even when we're thinking about the past or the future?" This, actually quite obvious, remark again brought on the sudden sensation of having no weight. At the same time, the present seemed to become a kind of moving stillness, an eternal stream from which neither I nor anything could deviate. I saw that everything, just as it is now, is IT— is the whole point of there being life and a universe. I saw that when the *Upanishads* said, "That art thou!" or "All this world is Brahman," they meant just exactly what they said. Each thing, each event, each experience in its inescapable nowness and in all its own particular individuality was precisely what it should be, and so much so that it acquired a divine authority and originality. It struck me with the fullest clarity that none of this depended on my seeing it to be so; that was the way things were, whether I understood it or not, and if I did not understand, that was IT too. Furthermore, I felt that I now understood what Christianity might mean by the love of God—namely, that despite the commonsensical imperfection of things, they were nonetheless loved by God just as they are, and that this loving of them was at the same time the godding of them. This time the vivid sensation of lightness and clarity lasted a full week.

These experiences, reinforced by others that have followed, have been the enlivening force of all my work in writing and in philosophy since that time, though I have come to realize that how I *feel*, whether the actual sensation of freedom and clarity is present or not, is not the point—for, again, to feel heavy or restricted is also IT. But with this point of departure a philosopher is faced with a strange problem of communication, especially to the degree that his philosophy seems to have some affinity with religion. People appear to be under the fixed impression that one speaks or writes of these things in order to improve them or do them some good, assuming, too, that the speaker has himself been improved and is able to speak with authority. In other words, the philosopher is forced into the role of preacher, and is in turn expected to practice what he preaches. Thereupon the truth of what he says is tested by his character and his morals—whether he shows anxiety or not, whether he depends upon "material crutches" such as wine or tobacco, whether he has stomach ulcers or likes money, whether he loses his temper, or gets depressed, or falls in love when he shouldn't, or sometimes looks a bit tired and frayed at the edges. All these criteria might be valid if the philosopher were preaching freedom from being human, or if he were trying to make himself and others radically better.

In the span of one lifetime it is, of course, possible for almost every human being to improve himself—within limits set by energy, time, temperament, and the level from which he begins. Obviously, then, there is a proper place for preachers and other technical advisers in the disciplines of human betterment. But the limits within which such improvements may be made are small in comparison with the vast aspects of our nature and our circumstances which remain the same, and which will be very difficult to improve even were it desirable to do so. I am saying, therefore, that while there is a place for bettering oneself and others, solving problems and coping with situations is by no means the only or even the chief business of life. Nor is it the principal work of philosophy.

Human purposes are pursued within an immense circling universe which does not seem to me to have purpose, in our sense, at all. Nature is much more playful than purposeful, and the probability that it has no special goals for the future need not strike one as a defect. On the contrary, the processes of nature as we see them both in the surrounding world and in the involuntary aspects of our own organisms are much more like art than like business, politics, or religion. They are especially like the arts of music and dancing, which unfold themselves without aiming at future destinations. No one imagines that a symphony is supposed to improve in quality as it goes along, or that the whole object of playing it is to reach the finale. The point of music is discovered in every moment of playing and listening to it. It is the same, I feel, with the greater part of our lives, and if we are unduly absorbed in improving them we may forget altogether to live them. The musician whose chief concern is to make every performance better than the last may so fail to participate and delight in his own music that he will impress his audience only with the anxious rigor of his technique.

Thus it is by no means the main work of a philosopher to be classed with the moralists and reformers. There is such a thing as philosophy, the love of wisdom, in the spirit of the artist. Such philosophy will not preach or advocate practices leading to improvement. As I understand it, the work of the philosopher as artist is to reveal and celebrate the eternal and purposeless background of human life. Out of simple exuberance or wonder he wants to tell others of the point of view from which the world is unimaginably good as it is, with people just as they are. No matter how difficult it may be to express this point of view without sounding smug or appearing to be a wishful dreamer, some hint of it may be suggested if the philosopher has had the good fortune to have experienced it himself.

This may sound like a purpose, like a desire to improve, to those who insist upon seeing all human activity in terms of goal-seeking. The trouble is that our Western common sense is firmly Artistotelian, and we therefore believe that the will never acts except for some good or pleasure. But upon analysis this turns out to say no more than that we do what we do, for if we *always* do what pleases us—even in committing suicide—there is no means of showing what pleases us apart from what we do. In using such logic I am only throwing a stone back to the glass house from which it came, for I am well aware that expressions of mystical experience will not stand the test of logic. But, unlike the Aristotelian, the mystic does not claim to be logical. His sphere of experience is the unspeakable. Yet this need mean no more than that it is the sphere of physical nature, of all that is not simply conceptions, numbers, or words.

If the experience of "cosmic consciousness" is unspeakable, it is true that in trying to utter it in words one is not "saying" anything in the sense of conveying information or making a proposition. The speech expressing such an experience is more like an exclamation. Or better, it is the speech of poetry rather than logic, though not poetry in the impoverished sense of the logical positivist, the sense of decorative and beautiful nonsense. For there is a kind of speech that may be able to convey something without actually being able to say it. Korzybski ran into this difficulty in trying to express the apparently simple point that things are not what we *say* they are, that, for example, the word "water" is not itself drinkable. He formulated it in his "law of nonidentity," that "whatever you say a thing *is*, it *isn't*." But from this it will follow that it isn't a thing either, for if I say that a thing is a thing, it isn't.

What, then, are we talking about? He was trying to show that we are talking about the unspeakable world of the physical universe, the world that is other than words. Words represent it, but if we want to *know* it directly we must do so by immediate sensory contact. What we call things, facts, or events are after all no more than convenient units of perception, recognizable pegs for names, selected from the infinite multitude of lines and surfaces, colors and textures, spaces and densities which surround us. There is no more a fixed and final way of dividing these variations into things than of grouping the stars in constellations.

From this example, however, it is certainly clear that we can point out the unspeakable world, and even convey the idea of its existence, without being able to say exactly *what* it is. We do not know what it is. We know only that it is. To be able to say what it is we must be able to classify it, but obviously the "all" in which the whole multiplicity of things is delineated cannot be classified.

The sphere of "cosmic consciousness" is, I believe, the same as the unspeakable world of Korzybski and the semanticists. It is nothing "spiritual" in the usual sense of abstract or ideational. It is concretely physical, yet for this very reason ineffable (or unspeakable) and indefinable. "Cosmic" consciousness is a release from self-consciousness, that is to say from the fixed belief and feeling that one's organism is an absolute and separate thing, as distinct from a convenient unit of perception. For if it becomes clear that our use of the lines and surfaces of nature to divide the world into units is only a matter of convenience, then all that I have called myself is actually inseparable from everything. This is exactly what one experiences in these extraordinary moments. It is not that the outlines and shapes which we *call* things and use to delineate things disappear into some sort of luminous void. It simply becomes obvious that though they may be used as divisions they do not really divide. However much I may be impressed by the difference between a star and the dark space around it, I must not forget that I can see the two only in relation to each other, and that this relation is inseparable.

The most astonishing feature of this experience is, however, the conviction that this entire unspeakable world is "right," so right that our normal anxieties become ludicrous, that if only men could see it they would go wild with joy,

> And the king be cutting capers,
> And the priest be picking flowers.

Quite apart from the difficulty of relating this sensation to the problem of evil and pain, there is the question of the very meaning of the assertion "All shall be well, and all shall be well, and all manner of thing shall be well." I can say only that the meaning of the assertion is the experience itself. Outside that state of consciousness it has no meaning, so much so that it would be difficult even to believe in it as a revelation without the actual experience. For the experience makes it perfectly clear that the whole universe is through and through the playing of love in every shade of the word's use, from animal lust to divine charity. Somehow this includes even the holocaust of the biological world, where every creature lives by feeding on others. Our usual picture of this world is reversed so that every victim is seen as offering itself in sacrifice.

If we are to ask whether this vision is true, we may first answer that there are no such things as truths by themselves: a truth is always in relation to a point of view. Fire is hot in relation to skin. The structure of the world appears as it does in relation to our organs of sense and our brains. Therefore certain alterations in the human organism may turn it into the sort of percipient for which the world *is* as it is seen in this vision. But, in the same way, other alterations will give us the truth of the world as it appears to the schizophrenic, or to the mind in black depression.

There is, however, a possible argument for the superior truth of the "cosmic" experience. Its basis is simply that no energy system can be completely self-controlling without ceasing to move. Control is restraint upon movement, and because complete control would be complete restraint, control must always be subordinate to motion if there is to be motion at all. In human terms, total restraint of movement is the equivalent of total doubt, of refusal to trust one's senses or feelings in any respect, and perhaps its embodiment is the extreme catatonic who refuses every motion or communication. On the other hand, movement and the release of restraint are the equivalent of faith, of committing oneself to the uncontrolled and unknown. In an extreme form this would mean the abandonment of oneself to utter caprice, and at first sight a life of such indiscriminate faith might seem to correspond to a vision of the world in which "everything is right." Yet this point of view would exclude all control as wrong, and thus there would be no place in it for the rightness of restraint. An essential part of the "cosmic" experience is, however, that the normal restriction of consciousness to the ego-feeling is also right, but only and always because it is subordinate to absence of restriction, to movement and faith.

The point is simply that, if there is to be any life and movement at all, the attitude of faith must be basic— the final and fundamental attitude—and the attitude of doubt secondary and subordinate. This is another way of saying that toward the vast and all-encompassing background of human life, with which the philosopher as artist is concerned, there must be total affirmation and acceptance. Otherwise there is no basis at all for caution and control with respect to details in the foreground. But it is all too easy to become so absorbed in these details that all sense of proportion is lost, and for man to make himself mad by trying to bring everything under his control. We become insane, unsound, and without foundation when we lose consciousness of and faith in the uncontrolled and ungraspable background world which is ultimately what we ourselves are. And there is a very slight distinction, if any, between complete, conscious faith and love.

2

INSTINCT, INTELLIGENCE, AND ANXIETY

From the moment of birth it is only a matter of weeks for little birds to fly, ducklings to swim, kittens to hunt and climb trees, and young monkeys to swing in the branches. Though these creatures live much shorter lives than men, proportionately it takes them only a fraction of the time required for the civilized human being to learn the essential arts of life. For them the mere fact of existence seems to guarantee the skills for survival, and one might almost say that its techniques are built into their bodies. But for human beings, survival in the context of a civilized community demands the mastery of an art of thinking, learning, and choosing which takes up about a quarter of the average span of life. Furthermore, it seems that living in a civilized society calls for a way of thinking and acting entirely different from the ways of animals, insects, and plants. Ordinarily this is called, rather vaguely, the way of intelligence as over against the way of instinct. The difference is roughly that action by instinct is spontaneous, whereas action by intelligence involves a difficult process of analysis, prediction, and decision.

Both forms of action are astonishingly skillful, though thus far it seems that the way of intelligence is the better guarantor of survival—at least in so far as its application in technology has increased our average life expectancy by some twenty years. But the gains of action by intelligence are bought at a price which at times seems so heavy that we might ask whether they are worth it. For the price of intelligence as we now know it is chronic anxiety, anxiety which appears to increase —oddly enough—to the very degree that human life is subjected to intelligent organization.

The type of intelligence that we have cultivated brings anxiety for at least three principal reasons. The first is that intelligent thinking works by dividing the world of experience into separate facts and events, simple enough for conscious attention to focus upon them one at a time. But there are innumerable ways of dividing and selecting for attention the facts and events, the data, required for any prediction or decision, and thus when the moment comes for a choice there is always the rankling doubt that important data may have been overlooked. There is therefore no complete assurance that an important decision is right. Thus the ever-frustrated effort to gain complete assurance by reviewing the data becomes the special anxiety which we call a sense of responsibility. The second is that the sense of responsibility goes hand in hand with a heightened sense of being an independent individual—a source of action which cannot *depend* upon simple instinct or spontaneity for doing the appropriate thing. The intelligent man therefore feels independent of or cut off from the rest of nature, and in trying, ever frustratedly, to figure nature out with sufficient accuracy he acquires a feeling of fear and hostility toward everything outside his own will and its full control. The third is that conscious attention reviews facts and events *in series*, even though they may be happening all together at once. Thinking about them in series and making predictions and decisions about the future course of the series gives the intelligent man a vivid awareness of *time.* It appears to him as a basic life process which he must work *against.* He knows that he must calculate rapidly to forestall it, though reviewing nature analytically, piece by piece, is not conducive to speed. Furthermore, knowledge of the future brings about emotional reactions to future events before they happen, and thus anxiety because, for example, one may get sick or will eventually die. And apparently this does not trouble the creatures who act by instinct.

Now action by intelligence is in a special and high degree characteristic of Western civilization, though other civilizations have developed it highly enough to experience the same problem of chronic anxiety. But Western civilization has acquired by far the greatest measure of skill in controlling the course of events by or-

ganized intelligence. Yet this appears to have intensi-
fied rather than abated our anxiety. For to the extent
that we have analyzed the natural world and the human world more thoroughly, to that extent it appears
to us to be more complicated. The scope of our detailed
information about the world is so vast that every individual, every responsible source of action, finds it too
great to master—without depending upon the collaboration of others who are, however, beyond his control.
Collaboration requires faith, but faith is an instinctual
attitude; speaking quite strictly, it is not intelligent to
trust what you have not analyzed.

It looks, then, as if there is conflict, contradiction,
and thus anxiety in the very nature of intelligence. As
an efficient though slow and laborious means of conscious control, it builds up a body of information too
complex to be grasped by its own method of reviewing
events and facts one after another in series. Machines
or other people must be trusted to assist: but how much
must one know, how many facts must one review, before deciding to accept a collaborator? Intelligence,
which is in some sense systematic doubt, cannot pro-
ceed very far without also having to embrace its polar
opposite—instinctual faith. So long as intelligence and
faith seem mutually exclusive this is an impossible contradiction, for to the degree that intelligence is systematic doubt it cannot trust *itself*. This is why lack of self-
confidence is the peculiar neurosis of civilized man, and
why he elaborates ever more complex arrangements for

legal safeguarding, foolproofing, and checking, double-checking, and triple-checking every decisive action. All of which leads to the kind of bureaucratic stalemate with which we are so familiar. (I recall a recent incident in a department of the University of California where it was impossible to spend twenty-five dollars on a supply typist without filling out a complex form with twelve carbons, four of which were illegible.)

Not only the anxiety but also the sheer stalemate and paralysis which often attend strictly intelligent and noninstinctual action are the more important causes of anti-intellectual movements in our society. It is through impatience and exasperation with such snarls that democracies vote themselves into dictatorships. It is in protest against the laborious unmanageability of vast technical knowledge in literature, painting, and music that writers and artists go berserk and break every rule in the name of sheer instinctual exuberance. It is in revolt against the insufferable heaps of unproductive paper-work that small businesses sell out to big corporations, and independent professional men take routine salaried jobs without responsibility. It is in disgust with the complex organization of the omnipotent registrar's office and the unimaginative pedantry of the Ph.D. course that people of real genius or creative ability are increasingly unable to work in our universities. It is also in despair of being able to understand or make any productive contribution to the highly organized chaos of our politico-economic system that large numbers of people simply abandon political and social commitments. They just let society be taken over by a pattern of organization which is as self-proliferative as a weed, and whose ends and values are neither human nor instinctual but mechanical. And we should note that a self-contradictory system of action breeds forms of revolt which are contradictory among themselves.

To some extent it is certainly a manifestation of this anti-intellectualism that there has recently been a marked increase of Western interest in the philosophies and religions of Asia. Unlike Christianity—for reasons which we shall explain—these are ways of life which seem, above all, to offer release from conflict and anxiety. Their goal is a state of inner feeling in which oppositions have become mutually co-operative instead of mutually exclusive, in which there is no longer any conflict between the individual man and nature, or between intelligence and instinct. Their view of the world is unitary (or, to be quite technical, "nondualistic"), and in such a world there is no absolute overwhelming urgency to be right rather than wrong, or to live rather than die. It is, however, quite difficult for us to understand this point of view, for the very reason that we habitually regard opposites as mutually exclusive, like God and the Devil. Because of this, our idea of unity and our way of solving conflicts is simply to eliminate one of the two parties. In other words, we have difficulty in seeing the relativity or mutual interdependence of contraries. For this reason our revolts against the excesses of intelligence are always in danger of selling out to instinct.

But this is the habitual dualist's solution to the problem of dualism: to solve the dilemma by chopping off one of the horns. At the same time, it is perhaps an understandable reaction to the conflict in which Western man has been placed by both Christianity and scientific rationalism. Christianity, even as it is understood by quite thoughtful Christians, is certainly no remedy for anxiety. In Christianity it matters not just very much but absolutely that one choose good rather than evil, for one's eternal destiny depends upon the decision. Yet to be certain that one is saved is the sin of presumption and to be certain that one is damned is the sin of despair. Likewise God as the rational principle of the universe stands on the side of intelligence rather than instinct, and particularly on the side of a humble or self-doubting intelligence—since man has been perverted by original sin in all his faculties, both animal and rational. To be contrite, repentant, and free from pride demands a constant and vigilant revival of the conflict between one's better half and one's innate perversity. This is certainly a heroic and energetically fact-facing discipline. But the more sensitively and wakefully it is pursued, the more one comes to a paralysis of the will. The facts of one's nature are discovered to be astoundingly complex and slippery, evil masquerading with endless subtlety as good, and construing the good as evil. And in this perplexity it still matters absolutely that one choose the good.

There are two obvious escapes from this dilemma. One is to stop being too keenly intelligent and too acutely conscious of the facts of one's inner life, and to fall back upon an inflexibly formal, traditional, and authoritarian pattern of thought and action—as if to say, "Just *do* the right thing, and don't be sophisticatedly psychological about your motives. Just obey, and don't ask questions." This is called sacrificing the pride of the intellect. But here we find ourselves in another dilemma, for the religion of simple obedience soon totters toward empty formalism and moral legalism with no heart in it, the very Pharisaism against which Christ railed. The other escape is into a romanticism of the instincts, a glorification of mere impulse ignoring the equally natural gift of will and reason. This is actually a modern form of the old practice of selling one's soul to the Devil—always a possible release from anxiety and conflict because damnation could at least be certain.

Hinduism and Buddhism have recognized that man's path is a razor's edge and that there is no real escape from the great conflicts of feeling and action. Yet, unlike most forms of Christianity, they do envisage, not an escape, but a resolution of the conflict within this present life. Their answer is, moreover, deceptively close to the "anything goes" attitude of instinctual romanticism—at least this is true of the more profound and inward forms of their doctrine, which are just those having so much appeal to the West. For they do indeed teach that good and evil, pleasure and pain, life and death are mutually interdependent, and that there is a Tao; a way of nature or a balance of nature, from which we can never actually deviate—however wrongly we may act from a limited point of view.

Yet their grasp of the mutuality of opposites is infinitely more thorough than that of our romanticist with his exclusive valuation of precipitate and uncalculated action. The difficult and subtle point which the romanticist misses and which, on the other extreme, the strict intellectual rationalist cannot understand at all, is that if *all* action and existence is in accord with the undeviating Tao or way of nature, no special means or methods are required to bring this accord into being. In the language of Zen, such means are "legs on a snake," or irrelevancies—and these include precisely the choice of impulsive rather than reflective and intelligent action. The romanticist advertises his ignorance of the Tao in the very act of trying to be spontaneous, and of preferring the so-called natural and instinctual to the artificial and intelligent.

To overcome the conflict between intelligence and instinct it is first necessary to understand, or at least imagine, a point of view, or perhaps a state of mind, which is experiential rather than intellectual—a kind of sensation rather than a set of ideas. When put into words, this sensation is always paradoxical, but in experience it is not paradoxical at all. Everyone who has felt it has always felt at the same time that it is totally simple and clear. However, I think the same is true of *all* our sensations. There seems to be no paradox in describing our more ordinary sensations because everyone has had them, and the listener always knows what you mean. There is no problem in understanding me when I say, "I see light because of the sun." But it is *also* true that the sun is light because I see—because, in other words, light is a *relationship* between the eyes and the sun, and the description of relationships always tends to sound paradoxical. When the earth collides with a meteor, we can say either that the meteor ran into the earth or that the earth ran into the meteor. Whichever we say depends upon an arbitrary frame of reference, and so both statements are true, even though apparently contradictory.

In the same way it is only *apparently* contradictory to describe a sensation in which it seems that whatever I do freely and intelligently is at the same time completely determined, and vice versa. It seems that absolutely everything both inside and outside me is happening by itself, yet at the same time that I myself am doing all of it, that my separate individuality is simply a function, something being done by everything which is not me, yet at the same time everything which is not me is a function of my separate individuality. Ordinarily we can see the truth of these seemingly paradoxical feelings if we take them separately, if we look at one without looking simultaneously at the other. This is why, for example, the arguments for free will and determinism are equally cogent though seemingly contradictory. The same goes for almost all the great debates of Western philosophy—the realists against the nominalists, the idealists against the materialists, and so on. We get into conflicts and debates about these problems because our language and our way of thinking are somewhat clumsy in their grasp of relationship. In other words, because it is much easier for us to see opposites as mutually exclusive than as mutually interdependent.

The sensation I am trying to describe is the experience of things and events in relationship, as distinct from the partial experience of things and events in separation. I have sometimes said that if we could translate the modern Western theory of relativity into experience, we should have what the Chinese and the Indians call the Absolute—as when they say that everything which happens is the Tao, or that all things are of one "suchness." What they mean is that all things are in relation, and thus that—considered simply by itself —no thing, no event, has any reality. There seem to be relatively few people, even in the civilizations of Asia, for whom relationship is an actual sensation, over and above a mere idea. The anxiety which comes about through the conflict of intelligence with instinct, of man as the conscious will with nature both in and around him, does not seem to me to have any solution unless we can actually feel relationship, unless it is a matter of clear sensation that as determined beings we are free, and that as free beings we are determined. For if we can *feel* this way, it will not appear that the use of will and intelligence is a conflict with our natural environment and endowment.

It is surely obvious that how you do things depends crucially upon how you feel. If you feel inwardly isolated from the natural world, your dealings with it will tend to be hostile and aggressive. It is not so much a matter of what you do as of how you do it, not so much the content as the style of action adopted. It is easy enough to see this in leading or persuading other people, for one and the same communication may have quite opposite results according to the style or feeling with which it is given. Yet this is equally true in dealing with inanimate nature and with our own inner nature—with our instincts and appetites. They will yield to intelligence much more agreeably to the extent that we feel ourselves to be one with them, or, to put it in another way, to be in relationship to them, to have the unity of mutual interdependence.

Furthermore, the sensation of relationship simply wipes out those special anxieties of the intelligence which come about as a result of the exaggerated feeling of individual responsibility of choice and of working against time. For this is the sensation which, however garbled and perverted, is the impulse underlying the great religious traditions of the world—the sensation of basic inseparability from the total universe, of the identity of one's own self with the Great Self beneath all that exists.

Why, then, do we not feel relationship? Why is the mutual interdependence between ourselves and the external world not the most obvious and dominant fact of consciousness? Why do we not see that the world we try to control, our whole inner and outer natural environment, is precisely that which gives us the power to control anything? It is because we look at things separately instead of simultaneously. When we are busy trying to control or change our circumstances, we ignore and are unconscious of the dependence of our consciousness and energy upon the outer world. When, on the other hand, we are oppressed by circumstances and feel controlled by the outer world, we forget that our very own consciousness is bringing that world into being. For, as I said, the sun is light because there are eyes to see it—noises because there are ears to hear them, hard facts because there is soft skin to feel them. But this is an unfamiliar point of view, and at once we disclaim it, saying, "Oh, but I didn't make my consciousness, my eyes, my ears, and my sensitive skin! They were given to me by my father and mother, or perhaps by God."

But should we not, then, make the same disclaimer when things are going well, and when the conscious intellect is busy pushing the universe around? Furthermore, if my consciousness is something which I do not fully control, something given to me by my parents, who or what is the "I" which "has" this consciousness? Who am I if not this consciousness which I have just disclaimed? Surely it is obvious that there is no sort of little man inside us who has or who owns this consciousness on trust. This is a figment of speech taken too seriously. If, therefore, consciousness ceases to ignore itself and becomes fully self-conscious, it discovers two things: (1) that it controls itself only very slightly, and is thoroughly dependent on other things—father and mother, external nature, biological processes, God, or what you will, and (2) that there is no little man inside, no "I" who owns this consciousness. And if that is so, if I do not own my consciousness, and if there is even no "me" to own it, to receive it, or to put up with it, who on earth is there to be either the victim of fate or the master of nature? "What is troubling us," said Wittgenstein, "is the tendency to believe that the mind is like a little man within."

Now if we examine the records of mystical experience, or of what I am now calling the experience of relationship, we shall find that, time and time again, it is connected with "spiritual poverty"—that is to say, with giving up the ownership of everything, including oneself or one's consciousness. It is the total abandonment of proprietorship on the external world of nature and the internal world of the human organism. This does not come about through the virtue of the will, through one's own strength, which in any case is not one's own. It comes about from the insight that there is no proprietor, no inner controller. This becomes evident as soon as the consciousness which has felt itself to be the inner controller starts to examine itself, and finds out that it does not give itself the power of control. Its push is nature's pull; it is a loop in an endless knot, where a pull from the right is a push from the left.

When it thus becomes clear that I own nothing, not even what I have called myself, it is as if, to use St. Paul's words, I had nothing but possessed all things. When I can no more identify myself with that little man inside, there is nothing left to identify with—except everything! There is no longer the slightest contradiction between feeling like a leaf on a stream and throwing one's whole energy into responsible action, for the push is the pull. And thus in using intelligence to change what has hitherto been the course of nature, one has the realization that this is a new bend in the course and that the whole flood of the stream is behind it.

All that I have been describing is a subjective feeling. It gives no specific direction as to what is or is not a proper use of intelligence in varying the course of nature—which must always be a matter of opinion and of trial and error. What it does give is what I feel to be a correct apprehension of the continuum, of the context, in which we are working, and this seems to me to be prior to, basic to, the problem of what exactly is to be done. Much as we discuss the latter question, is it really sensible to do so until we are more aware of the context in which action is to be taken? That context is our relationship to the whole so-called objective world of nature—and relationship as something concrete, as more than an abstract and theoretical positioning of billiard balls, is practically screened out of consciousness by our present use of intelligence.

Just as the study of natural history was first an elaborate classification of the separate species and only recently involved ecology, the study of the interrelation of species, so intelligence as a whole is at first no more than a division of the world into things and events. This overstresses the independence and separateness of things, and of ourselves from them, as things among things. It is the later task of intelligence to appreciate the inseparable relationships between the things so divided, and so to rediscover the universe as distinct from a mere multiverse. In so doing it will see its own limitations, see that intelligence alone is not enough—that it cannot operate, cannot *be* intelligence, without an approach to the world through instinctual feeling with its possibility of *knowing* relationship as you know when you drink it that water is cold.

3

ZEN AND THE PROBLEM
OF CONTROL

As we now know him, the human being seems to be a trap set to catch himself. Though this has doubtless been true for thousands of years, it has recently been accentuated in a peculiar way by man's sudden development, through science and technology, of so many new means of controlling himself and his environment. In the early days of modern science the situation was less obvious, for the application of scientific controls to nature and to ourselves seemed to be something that we could extend indefinitely along wide and unobstructed roads. But today, after the Second World War and past the middle of the twentieth century, the snag in the problem of control is beginning to make itself obvious in almost every field of man's activity. It is, perhaps, at its very clearest in the sciences of communication which include study of the dynamics of control, and also in psychology, the science which deals most intimately with man himself.

In its simplest and most basic form—of which all its other forms are just extensions and exaggerations—the problem is this: man is a self-conscious and therefore self-controlling organism, but how is he to control the aspect of himself which does the controlling? All attempts to solve this problem seem to end in a snarl, whether at the individual level or at the social. At the individual level the snarl manifests itself in what we call acute self-consciousness, as when a public speaker frustrates himself by his very effort to speak well. At the social level it manifests itself as a loss in freedom of movement increasing with every attempt to regulate action by law. In other words, there is a point beyond which self-control becomes a form of paralysis—as if I wanted simultaneously to throw a ball and hold it to its course with my hand.

Technology, which increases the power and range of human control, at the same time increases the intensity of these snarls. The apparent multiplication of psychological disorders in our technological culture is perhaps due to the fact that more and more individuals find themselves caught in these snarls—in situations which the psychiatric anthropologist Gregory Bateson has called the "double-bind" type, where the individual is required to make a decision which at the same time he cannot or must not make. He is called upon, in other words, to do something contradictory, and this is usually within the sphere of self-control, the sort of contradiction epitomized in the title of a well-known book,

You Must Relax. Need it be said that the demand for effort in "must" is inconsistent with the demand for effortlessness in "relax"?

Now it is of great interest that we cannot effectively think about self-control without making a separation between the controller and the controlled, even when—as the word "self-control" implies—the two are one and the same. This lies behind the widespread conception of man as a double or divided being composed of a higher self and a lower, of reason and instinct, mind and body, spirit and matter, voluntary and involuntary, angel and animal. So conceived, man is never actually self-controlling. It is rather that one part of his being controls another, so that what is required of the controlling part is that it exert its fullest effort and otherwise be freely and uninhibitedly itself. And the conception is all very well—until it fails. Then who or what is to blame? Was the lower, controlled self too strong, or was the higher, controlling self too weak? If the former, man as the controller cannot be blamed. If the latter, something must be done to correct the weakness. But this means, in other words, that the higher, controlling self must control *itself*—or else we must posit a still higher self available to step in and control the controller. Yet this can go on forever.

The problem is well illustrated in the Christian theory of virtue, which for centuries has put an immense double-bind on Western man. The greatest commandment is that "Thou *shalt* love the Lord thy God"—and, note the addition—"with *all* thy heart, and *all* thy soul, and *all* thy mind." How can such a commandment be obeyed? The addition implies that it is not enough to think and act *as if* I loved God. I am not asked to pretend that I love. I am asked really to mean it, to be completely sincere. Jesus' whole condemnation of the Parisees was that they obeyed the law of God insincerely —with their lips and hands, but not with their hearts. But, if the heart is the controller, how is it to convert itself? If I am to love sincerely, I must love with my whole being, with unhindered spontaneity. But this amounts to saying that I *must* be spontaneous, and controlled or willed spontaneity is a contradiction!

Christian theology has attempted to clarify the problem by saying that the heart cannot convert itself without the help of God, without divine grace, a power that descends from above to control the controller. But this has never been a solution because it is really a postponement of the solution, or a repetition of the same problem at another level. For if I am commanded to love God, and if obeying the commandment requires God's grace, then I am commanded to get God's grace. Once again, I am commanded to control the controller who, in this case, is God. Or to put it in still other terms, I am commanded to lay myself open to the influence of God's grace. But will I truly lay myself open if I do it halfheartedly? And if I have to do it wholeheartedly, must I not have the grace to lay myself open to grace? This, too, can go on forever.

The point which emerges here is that the problem of self-control is not made any clearer, but rather the contrary, by splitting the self into two parts—and it matters not whether the self in question be the human organism or the whole universe. This is why all types of dualistic philosophy are ultimately unsatisfactory, even though we do not seem to be able to think effectively about problems of control without resorting to dualism. For if the human organism does not have a separate controlling part, if the higher self is simply the same as the lower, self-control must seem to our dualistic way of thinking as impossible as trying to make a finger point at its own tip. We might argue that self-control is an illusion and that man's organism is a completely determined machine. But the argument is actually self-contradictory. For when a machine states that it *is* a machine, it is presuming that it is able to observe itself—and once again we have the apparent absurdity of the finger pointing at itself. In other words, to assert that I am not capable of self-control at once implies a measure of self-knowledge, self-observation, and, to that degree, of self-control. The human predicament seems to be a trap whichever way we look at it—if to deny one's self-consciousness is to assert it, and if to assert it, as seems inevitable, is to be caught in a paradox and involved in a double-bind.

The division of man into higher and lower selves does not clarify the problem of self-control, because it remains a useful description of the dynamics of control only so long as the (higher) will *succeeds* in mastering the (lower) feelings. But when the will fails and needs somehow to strengthen itself or transform itself from ill-will to good, the dualistic description of man is not only useless but confusing. For it is a way of thinking which divides man from himself at the very moment when he needs "to get with himself." That is to say, when the will is struggling with itself and is in conflict with itself it is paralyzed, like a person trying to walk in two opposite directions at once. At such moments the will has to be released from its paralysis in rather the same way that one turns the front wheel of a bicycle in the direction in which one is falling. Surprisingly, to the beginner, one does not lose control but regains it. The moralist, like the beginning bicyclist, can never believe that turning to the direction in which one's will is falling will bring about anything but a complete moral fall. Yet the unexpected psychological fact is that man cannot control himself unless he accepts himself. In other words, before he can change his course of action he must first be sincere, going with and not against his nature, even when the immediate trend of his nature is toward evil, toward a fall. The same is true in sailing a boat, for when you want to sail against the direction of the wind, you do not invite conflict by turning straight into the wind. You tack against it, keeping the wind in your sails. So, also, in order to recover himself the automobile driver must turn in the direction of a skid.

Our problem is that our long indoctrination in dualistic thinking has made it a matter of common sense that we can control our nature only by going against it. But this is the same false common sense which urges the driver to turn against the skid. To maintain control we have to learn new reactions, just as in the art of *judo* one must learn not to resist a fall or an attack but to control it by swinging with it. Now *judo* is a direct application to wrestling of the Zen and Taoist philosophy of *wu-wei*, of *not asserting* oneself against nature, of not being in frontal opposition to the direction of things. The objective of the Zen way of life is the experience of awakening or enlightenment (insight, we should say in current psychological jargon), in which man escapes from the paralysis, the double-bind, in which the dualistic idea of self-control and self-consciousness involves him. In this experience man overcomes his feeling of dividedness or separateness—not only from himself as the higher controlling self against the lower controlled self, but also from the total universe of other people and things. The interest of Zen is that it provides a uniquely simple and classic example of a way of recognizing and dissolving the conflict or contradiction of self-consciousness.

The student of Zen is confronted by a master who has himself experienced awakening, and is in the best sense of the expression a completely natural man. For the adept in Zen is one who manages to be human with the same artless grace and absence of inner conflict with which a tree is a tree. Such a man is likened to a ball in a mountain stream, which is to say that he cannot be blocked, stopped, or embarrassed in any situation. He never wobbles or dithers in his mind, for though he may pause in overt action to think a problem out, the stream of his consciousness always moves straight ahead without being caught in the vicious circles of anxiety or indecisive doubt, wherein thought whirls wildly around without issue. He is not precipitate or hurried in action, but simply continuous. This is what Zen means by being detached—not being without emotion or feeling, but being one in whom feeling is not sticky or blocked, and through whom the experiences of the world pass like the reflections of birds flying over water. Although possessed of complete inner freedom, he is not, like the libertine, in revolt against social standards, nor, like the self-righteous, trying to justify himself. He is all of a piece with himself and with the natural world, and in his presence you feel that without strain or artifice he is completely "all here"—sure of himself without the slightest trace of aggression. He is thus the *grand seigneur*, the spiritual aristocrat comparable to the type of worldly aristocrat who is so sure of the position given to him by birth that he has no need to condescend or put on airs.

Confronted by such an example, the ordinary Zen student feels totally uncouth and ill at ease—particularly because his situation *as* student requires him to try to respond to the master with the same unhesitating and unself-conscious naturalness. Worse still, the gambits to which he must respond are *koans* or problem-questions which are designed to plunk him straight into double-bind situations. A typical *koan* is, "Show me your original face which you had before your father and mother conceived you!" Show me—in other words—your genuine, deepest self, not the self which depends on family and conditioning, on learning or experience, or any kind of artifice.

Obviously, a consciously planned and thought-out answer will not do, for this will spring from the student's culturally conditioned ego, from the personal role which he is playing. Thus no deliberate or willed response will answer the problem, since this will show only the acquired self. On the other hand, the only alternative under the circumstances will be for the student to try to make a response which is wholly spontaneous and unpremeditated. But here is the double-bind. Just *try* to be natural! A student once asked one of the old Chinese masters, "What is the Way?" He replied, "Your ordinary [that is, natural] mind is the Way." "How," continued the student, "am I to accord with it?" "When you *try* to accord with it," said the master, "you deviate from it." This means, too, that it will be no good for the student *not* to try, for this will still be intentional and thus an indirect way of trying. Under these circumstances most students are nonplussed and blocked for a considerable length of time, for when asked to act without controlling themselves they are *faced* with their own acting and existing and so paralyzed by self-consciousness.

In this predicament, the student discovers that so long as he is aware of himself he cannot—obviously—be unself-conscious. When he tries to forget himself, he remembers that *he* is trying to forget. On the other hand, when he does forget himself by absorption in everyday affairs, he finds that he is carried away by affairs and that he is responding to them not spontaneously but by socially conditioned habit. He is just unconsciously acting his role, and still not showing his original face. The master will not let him escape into this unconsciousness, for every confrontation with the student reminds him painfully of his awkward self. By these means the student is at last convinced that his ego, the self which he has believed himself to be, is nothing but a pattern of habits or artificial reactions. Strain as it will, there is nothing it can do to be natural, to let go of itself.

At this point the student feels himself to be a complete and abject failure. His acquired personality, his learning and knowledge seem—at least for this purpose—worthless. Hitherto, be it remembered, he has been trying—or trying not to try—to show his genuine self, to act in perfect sincerity. He now knows beyond any shadow of doubt that *he* cannot do it; somehow it must happen by itself. He finds, then, that he has no alternative but to be, to accept, the awkward, self-conscious, and conditioned creature that he is. But here, too, he runs into an apparent contradiction. For the idea of accepting oneself is another double-bind. Oneself includes conflicts—objections and resistances to oneself—and thus one is asked to accept one's not-accepting. Let your mind alone; let it think whatever it likes. But one of the things it likes is interfering with itself. Or look at it the other way around. As a Zen student he has been meditating, spending hours trying to keep his mind still, concentrating only on the *koan* or on his breathing, and cutting out distracting thoughts. But this is the blind leading the blind, for the mind that needs to be controlled is the one that does the controlling. Thought is trying to drive out thought.

At this moment there is a sudden flash of psychological lightning. What should have been obvious all the time has leaped into full clarity, and the student runs to his master and, without the least difficulty, shows him his "original face." What happened? All this time the student had been paralyzed by the ingrained conviction that he was one thing, and his mind, or thoughts, or sensations, another. Thus when faced with himself, he had always felt split in two—unable to show himself all of a piece, without contradiction. But now it has suddenly become a self-evident feeling that there is no separate thinker who "has" or who controls the thoughts. Thinker and thoughts are the same. After all, if you begin to let your mind think what it likes, the next moment it wants to interfere with itself, so let it do that. So long as you let it think what it wants at each successive moment, there is absolutely no effort, no difficulty, in letting it go. But the disappearance of the effort to let go is precisely the disappearance of the separate thinker, of the ego trying to watch the mind without interfering. Now there is nothing to try to do, for whatever comes up moment by moment is accepted, including not-accepting. For a second the thinker seems to be responding to the flow of thought with the immediacy of a mirror image, and then suddenly it dawns that there is no mirror and no image. There is simply the flow of thought—one after another without interference—and the mind really knows *itself*. There is no separate mind which stands aside and looks at it.

Furthermore, when the dualism of thinker and thought disappears so does that of subject and object. The individual no more feels himself to be standing back from his sensations of the external world, just as he is no longer a thinker standing back from his thoughts. He therefore has a vivid sense of himself as identical with what he sees and hears, so that his subjective impression comes into accord with the physical fact that man is not so much an organism *in* an environment as an organism-environment relationship. The relationship is, as it were, more real than its two terms, somewhat as the inner unity of a stick is more solid than the difference of its two ends.

The human being who has realized this unity is no longer a trap set to catch itself. For self-consciousness is no more a state of being in two minds, which, fortuitously enough, also means a state of indecision and dither and psychic paralysis. This is what self-consciousness becomes when we try to handle it dualistically, taking as real the conventions of thought and speech which separate "I" from "myself," as well as mind from body, spirit from matter, knower from known. In separation, the self I know is never the one I need to know, and the one I control is never the one I need to control. Politically, this dualism is manifested in the separation of the government or the state from the people, which occurs even in a democracy, a supposedly self-governing community. But governments and states have to exist when people have no inner feeling of their solidarity with others, when human society is nothing more than an abstract term for a collection of individuals—divided from each other because each one is divided from himself.

In the Eastern world, Zen and other means of setting man free from his own clutches have been the concern only of small minorities. In the West, where we believe in, or are at least committed to, the dissemination of knowledge to all, we have no Zen masters with whom to study. Yet in this we may have an advantage, for the separation of master from student is another form of the duality of the controller and the controlled which—obviously—would not have to exist if the organism-environment called man were truly self-controlling. This is why, in Zen, the master does not actually teach the student anything, but forces him to find out for himself, and, furthermore, does not think of himself as a master, since it is only from the standpoint of the unawakened student that there are masters. We are forced to find out for ourselves, not by masters, but by their absence, so that there is no temptation for us to lean on others. It is true that the Japanese Zen student has the presence of the master's naturalness to embarrass him. But cannot we be embarrassed by our very natural environment of sky, earth, and water, as by the marvel of our own bodies, into making a response, into acting in a way that is commensurate with their splendor? Or must we continue to buffet them blindly with bulldozers, fancying ourselves as the independent controllers and conquerors of what is, after all, the greater and perhaps better half of ourselves?

It is not my purpose here, nor is it really in the spirit of this whole point of view, to indicate the specific things which should be done to bring about some technological application of this new feeling of man's relation to nature, both within and without his own organism. For what is important is not the particular things to be done but the attitude—the inner feeling and disposition—of the doer. What is needed is not a new kind of technique but a new kind of man, for as an old Taoist text says, "When the wrong man uses the right means, the right means work in the wrong way." And the task of developing a new kind of man is not as difficult as it seems once we are disabused of the idea that self-change and self-control are no more a matter of conflict between higher and lower natures, of good intentions against recalcitrant instincts. The problem is to overcome the ingrained disbelief in the power of winning nature by love, in the gentle (*ju*) way (*do*) of turning with the skid, of controlling ourselves by co-operating with ourselves.

4

BEAT ZEN, SQUARE ZEN, AND ZEN

NOTE

The following essay first appeared in the Chicago Review *for the Summer of 1958, and was later issued as a pamphlet by City Lights Books in San Francisco, to which certain additions were made, because this seemed to be a good context in which to discuss the influence of Zen on Western art, and because the original was published before the appearance of Kerouac's* Dharma Bums. *The present version contains some further additions and amendments.*

I had supposed that the original version of this essay had made my own position with respect to "Beat Zen" and "Square Zen" perfectly clear. It was, of course, obvious that I was not using the word "square" as a taunt since I was not speaking from the standpoint of "beat." But as a result of Stephen Mahoney's article "The Prevalence of Zen" which appeared in The Nation in October, 1958, the impression has been circulating that I am a spokesman for "Square Zen." By this term I was designating the traditional and official Zen schools of Japan, Rinzai and Soto, to which many Westerners do indeed belong. I do not, nor do I represent them in any capacity. This is not because I disrespect them or have some quarrel with them, but because in matters of this kind I am temperamentally not a joiner. I do not even style myself a Zen Buddhist. For the aspect of Zen in which I am personally interested is nothing that can be organized, taught, transmitted, certified, or wrapped up in any kind of system. It can't even be followed, for everyone has to find it for himself. As Plotinus said, it is "a flight of the alone to the Alone," and as an old Zen poem says:

> If you do not get it from yourself,
> Where will you go for it?

Fundamentally, this is in a sense the position of the whole Zen Buddhist tradition. Strictly speaking, there are no Zen masters because Zen has nothing to teach. From the earliest times those who have experienced Zen have always repulsed would-be disciples, not just to test their sincerity, but to give fair warning that the experience of awakening (satori) is not to be found by seeking, and is not in any case something that can be acquired or cultivated. But seekers have persistently refused to take this "No!" for an answer, and to this the Zen sages have responded with a kind of judo. Realizing the uselessness of just telling the seeker that seeking will not find, they have replied with counterquestions (koan) which have the effect of exciting the effort of seeking until it explodes with its own force, so that the student realizes the folly of seeking for himself—not just verbally but through to the very marrow of his bones. At this point the student "has" Zen. He knows himself to be one with all, for he is no longer separating himself from the universe by seeking something from it.

On the surface, this looks like a master-disciple relationship. But essentially it is what Buddhists call upaya or "skillful means," sometimes known as "giving a yellow leaf to a child to stop it crying for gold." In the course of centuries, however, the process of refusal and counterquestioning has become increasingly formal. Temples and institutions have arisen where it may be carried on, and these have in *turn created problems of ownership, administration, and discipline compelling Zen Buddhism to assume the form of a traditional hierarchy. In the Far East this has gone on for so long that it is part of the landscape, and some of its disadvantages are offset by the fact that it seems perfectly natural. There is nothing exotic or "special" about it. Even organizations can grow naturally. But it seems to me that the transplantation of this style of Zen to the West would be completely artificial. It would simply become another of the numerous cult organizations with their spiritual claims, vested interests, and "in-groups" of followers, with the additional disadvantage of the snob appeal of being a "very esoteric" form of Buddhism. Let Zen soak into the West informally, like the drinking of tea. We can digest it better that way.*

It is as difficult for Anglo-Saxons as for the Japanese to absorb anything quite so Chinese as Zen. For though the word "Zen" is Japanese and though Japan is now its home, Zen Buddhism is the creation of T'ang dynasty China. I do not say this as a prelude to harping upon the incommunicable subtleties of alien cultures. The point is simply that people who feel a profound need to justify themselves have difficulty in understanding the viewpoints of those who do not, and the Chinese who created Zen were the same kind of people as Lao-tzu, who, centuries before, had said, "Those who justify themselves do not convince." For the urge to make or prove oneself right has always jiggled the Chinese sense of the ludicrous, since as both Confucians and Taoists —however different these philosophies in other ways— they have invariably appreciated the man who can "come off it." To Confucius it seemed much better to be human-hearted than righteous, and to the great Taoists,

Lao-tzu and Chuang-tzu, it was obvious that one could not be right without also being wrong, because the two were as inseparable as back and front. As Chuang-tzu said, "Those who would have good government without its correlative misrule, and right without its correlative wrong, do not understand the principles of the universe."

To Western ears such words may sound cynical, and the Confucian admiration of "reasonableness" and compromise may appear to be a weak-kneed lack of commitment to principle. Actually they reflect a marvellous understanding and respect for what we call the balance of nature, human and otherwise—a universal vision of life as the Tao or way of nature in which the good and the evil, the creative and the destructive, the wise and the foolish are the inseparable polarities of existence. "Tao," said the *Chung-yung,* "is that from which one cannot depart. That from which one can depart is not the Tao." Therefore wisdom did not consist in trying to wrest the good from the evil but in learning to "ride" them as a cork adapts itself to the crests and troughs of the waves. At the roots of Chinese life there is a trust in the good-and-evil of one's own nature which is peculiarly foreign to those brought up with the chronic uneasy conscience of the Hebrew-Christian cultures. Yet it was always obvious to the Chinese that a man who mistrusts himself cannot even trust his mistrust, and must therefore be hopelessly confused.

For rather different reasons, Japanese people tend to

be as uneasy in themselves as Westerners, having a sense of social shame quite as acute as our more metaphysical sense of sin. This was especially true of the class most attracted to Zen, the *samurai*. Ruth Benedict, in that very uneven work *Chrysanthemum and Sword*, was, I think, perfectly correct in saying that the attraction of Zen to the *samurai* class was its power to get rid of an extremely awkward self-consciousness induced in the education of the young. Part and parcel of this self-consciousness is the Japanese compulsion to compete with oneself—a compulsion which turns every craft and skill into a marathon of self-discipline. Although the attraction of Zen lay in the possibility of liberation from self-consciousness, the Japanese version of Zen fought fire with fire, overcoming the "self observing the self" by bringing it to an intensity in which it exploded. How remote from the regimen of the Japanese Zen monastery are the words of the great T'ang master Lin-chi:

> In Buddhism there is no place for using effort. Just be ordinary and nothing special. Eat your food, move your bowels, pass water, and when you're tired go and lie down. The ignorant will laugh at me, but the wise will understand.

Yet the spirit of these words is just as remote from a kind of Western Zen which would employ this philosophy to justify a very self-defensive Bohemianism.

There is no single reason for the extraordinary growth of Western interest in Zen during the last twenty years

The appeal of Zen arts to the "modern" spirit in the West, the work of Suzuki, the war with Japan, the itchy fascination of "Zen stories," and the attraction of a non-conceptual, experiential philosophy in the climate of scientific relativism—all these are involved. One might mention, too, the affinities between Zen and such purely Western trends as the philosophy of Wittgenstein, Existentialism, General Semantics, the metalinguistics of B. L. Whorf, and certain movements in the philosophy of science and in psychotherapy. Always in the background there is our vague disquiet with the artificiality or "antinaturalness" of both Christianity, with its politically ordered cosmology, and technology, with its imperialistic mechanization of a natural world from which man himself feels strangely alien. For both reflect a psychology in which man is identified with a conscious intelligence and will standing apart from nature to control it, like the architect-God in whose image this version of man is conceived. The disquiet arises from the suspicion that our attempt to master the world from outside is a vicious circle in which we shall be condemned to the perpetual insomnia of controlling controls and supervising supervision ad infinitum.

To the Westerner in search of the reintegration of man and nature there is an appeal far beyond the merely sentimental in the naturalism of Zen—in the landscapes of Ma-yuan and Sesshu, in an art which is simultaneously spiritual and secular, which conveys the mystical in terms of the natural, and which, indeed, never even imagined a break between them. Here is a view of the world imparting a profoundly refreshing sense of wholeness to a culture in which the spiritual and the material, the conscious and the unconscious, have been cataclysmically split. For this reason the Chinese humanism and naturalism of Zen intrigue us much more strongly than Indian Buddhism or Vedanta. These, too, have their students in the West, but their followers seem for the most part to be displaced Christians—people in search of a more plausible philosophy than Christian supernaturalism to carry on the essentially Christian search for the miraculous. The ideal man of Indian Buddhism is clearly a superman, a yogi with absolute mastery of his own nature, according perfectly with the science-fiction ideal of "men beyond mankind." But the Buddha or awakened man of Chinese Zen is "ordinary and nothing special"; he is humorously human like the Zen tramps portrayed by Mu-ch'i and Liang-k'ai. We like this because here, for the first time, is a conception of the holy man and sage who is not impossibly remote, not superhuman but fully human, and, above all, not a solemn and sexless ascetic. Furthermore, in Zen the *satori* experience of awakening to our "original inseparability" with the universe seems, however elusive, always just around the corner. One has even met people to whom it has happened, and they are no longer mysterious occultists in the Himalayas or skinny yogis in cloistered ashrams. They are just like us, and yet much more at home in the world, floating much more easily upon the ocean of transience and insecurity.

Above all, I believe that Zen appeals to many in the post-Christian West because it does not preach, moralize, and scold in the style of Hebrew-Christian prophetism. Buddhism does not deny that there is a relatively limited sphere in which human life may be improved by art and science, reason and good will. However, it regards this sphere of activity as important but nonetheless subordinate to the comparatively limitless sphere in which things are as they are, always have been, and always will be—a sphere entirely beyond the categories of good and evil, success and failure, and individual health and sickness. On the one hand, this is the sphere of the great universe. Looking out into it at night, we make no comparisons between right and wrong stars, nor between well and badly arranged constellations. Stars are by nature big and little, bright and dim. Yet the whole thing is a splendor and a marvel which sometimes makes our flesh creep with awe. On the other hand, this is also the sphere of human, everyday life which we might call existential.

For there is a standpoint from which human affairs are as much beyond right and wrong as the stars, and from which our deeds, experiences, and feelings can no more be judged than the ups and downs of a range of mountains. Though beyond moral and social valuation, this level of human life may also be seen to be just as marvellous and uncanny as the great universe itself. This feeling may become particularly acute when the indiviudal ego tries to fathom its own nature, to plumb the inner sources of its own actions and consciousness. For here it discovers a part of itself—the inmost and greatest part—which is strange to itself and beyond its understanding and control. Odd as it may sound, the ego finds that its own center and nature is beyond itself. The more deeply I go into myself, the more I am not myself, and yet this is the very heart of me. Here I find my own inner workings functioning of themselves, spontaneously, like the rotation of the heavenly bodies and the drifting of the clouds. Strange and foreign as this aspect of myself at first seems to be, I soon realize that it *is* me, and much more me than my superficial ego. This is not fatalism or determinism, because there is no longer anyone being pushed around or determined; there is nothing that this deep "I" is not doing. The configuration of my nervous system, like the configuration of the stars, happens of itself, and this "itself" is the real "myself."

From this standpoint—and here language reveals its limitations with a vengeance—I find that I cannot help doing and experiencing, quite freely, what is always "right," in the sense that the stars are always in their "right" places. As Hsiang-yen put it,

> There's no use for artificial discipline,
> For, move as I will, I manifest the ancient Tao.

At this level, human life is beyond anxiety, for it can never make a mistake. If we live, we live; if we die, we die; if we suffer, we suffer; if we are terrified, we are terrified. There is no problem about it. A Zen master was once asked, "It is terribly hot, and how shall we escape the heat?" "Why not," he answered, "go to the place where it is neither hot nor cold?" "Where is that place?" "In summer we sweat; in winter we shiver." In Zen one does not feel guilty about dying, or being afraid, or disliking the heat. At the same time, Zen does not insist upon this point of view as something which one *ought* to adopt; it does not preach it as an ideal. For if you don't understand it, your very not-understanding is also IT. There would be no bright stars without dim stars, and, without the surrounding darkness, no stars at all.

The Hebrew-Christian universe is one in which moral urgency, the anxiety to be right, embraces and penetrates everything. God, the Absolute itself, is good as against bad, and thus to be immoral or in the wrong is to feel oneself an outcast not merely from human society but also from existence itself, from the root and ground of life. To be in the wrong therefore arouses a metaphysical anxiety and sense of guilt—a state of eternal damnation—utterly disproportionate to the crime. This metaphysical guilt is so insupportable that it must eventually issue in the rejection of God and of his laws—which is just what has happened in the whole movement of modern secularism, materialism, and naturalism. Absolute morality is profoundly destructive of morality, for the sanctions which it invokes against evil are far, far too heavy. One does not cure the headache by cutting off the head. The appeal of Zen, as of other forms of Eastern philosophy, is that it unveils behind the urgent realm of good and evil a vast region of oneself about which there need be no guilt or recrimination, where at last the self is indistinguishable from God.

But the Westerner who is attracted by Zen and who would understand it deeply must have one indispensable qualification: he must understand his own culture so thoroughly that he is no longer swayed by its premises unconsciously. He must really have come to terms with the Lord God Jehovah and with his Hebrew-Christian conscience so that he can take it or leave it without fear or rebellion. He must be free of the itch to justify himself. Lacking this, his Zen will be either "beat" or "square," either a revolt from the culture and social order or a new form of stuffiness and respectability. For Zen is above all the liberation of the mind from conventional thought, and this is something utterly different from rebellion against convention, on the one hand, or adapting foreign conventions, on the other.

Conventional thought is, in brief, the confusion of the concrete universe of nature with the conceptual things, events, and values of linguistic and cultural symbolism. For in Taoism and Zen the world is seen as an inseparably interrelated field or continuum, no part of which can actually be separated from the rest or valued above or below the rest. It was in this sense that Hui-neng, the Sixth Patriarch, meant that "fundamentally not one thing exists," for he realized that things are *terms*, not entities. They exist in the abstract world of thought, but not in the concrete world of nature. Thus one who actually perceives or feels this to be so no longer feels that he is an ego, except by definition. He sees that his ego is his *persona* or social role, a somewhat arbitrary selection of experiences with which he has been taught to identify himself. (Why, for example, do we say "I think" but not "I am beating my heart"?) Having seen this, he continues to play his social role without being taken in by it. He does not precipitately adopt a new role or play the role of having no role at all. He plays it cool.

The "beat" mentality as I am thinking of it is something much more extensive and vague than the hipster life of New York and San Francisco. It is a younger generation's nonparticipation in "the American Way of Life," a revolt which does not seek to change the existing order but simply turns away from it to find the significance of life in subjective experience rather than objective achievement. It contrasts with the "square" and other-directed mentality of beguilement by social convention, unaware of the correlativity of right and wrong, of the mutual necessity of capitalism and communism to each other's existence, of the inner identity of puritanism and lechery, or of, say, the alliance of church lobbies and organized crime to maintain laws against gambling.

Beat Zen is a complex phenomenon. It ranges from a use of Zen for justifying sheer caprice in art, literature, and life to a very forceful social criticism and "digging of the universe" such as one may find in the poetry of Ginsberg, Whalen, and Snyder, and, rather unevenly, in Kerouac, who is always a shade too self-conscious, too subjective, and too strident to have the flavor of Zen.

When Kerouac gives his philosophical final statement, "I don't know. I don't care. And it doesn't make any difference"—the cat is out of the bag, for there is a hostility in these words which clangs with self-defense. But just because Zen truly surpasses convention and its values, it has no need to say "To hell with it," nor to underline with violence the fact that anything goes.

It is indeed the basic intuition of Zen that there is an ultimate standpoint from which "anything goes." In the celebrated words of the master Yun-men, "Every day is a good day." Or as is said in the *Hsin-hsin Ming:*

> If you want to get the plain truth,
> Be not concerned with right and wrong.
> The conflict between right and wrong
> Is the sickness of the mind.

But this standpoint does not exclude and is not hostile toward the distinction between right and wrong at other levels and in more limited frames of reference. The world is seen to be beyond right and wrong when it is not framed: that is to say, when we are not looking at a particular situation by itself—out of relation to the rest of the universe. Within this room there is a clear difference between up and down; out in interstellar space there is not. Within the conventional limits of a human community there are clear distinctions between good and evil. But these disappear when human affairs are seen as part and parcel of the whole realm of nature. Every framework sets up a restricted field of relationships, and restriction is law or rule.

Now a skilled photographer can point his camera at almost any scene or object and create a marvellous composition by the way in which he frames and lights it. An unskilled photographer attempting the same thing creates only messes, for he does not know how to place the frame, the border of the picture, where it will be in relation to the contents. How eloquently this demonstrates that as soon as we introduce a frame anything does *not* go. But every work of art involves a frame. A frame of some kind is precisely what distinguishes a painting, a poem, a musical composition, a play, a dance, or a piece of sculpture from the rest of the world. Some artists may argue that they do not want their works to be distinguishable from the total universe, but if this be so they should not frame them in

galleries and concert halls. Above all they should not
sign them nor sell them. This is as immoral as selling
the moon or signing one's name to a mountain. (Such
an artist may perhaps be forgiven if he knows what he
is doing, and prides himself inwardly, not on being a
poet or painter, but a competent crook.) Only destructive little boys and vulgar excursionists go around ini-
tialling the trees.

Today there are Western artists avowedly using Zen
to justify the indiscriminate framing of simply anything
—blank canvases, totally silent music, torn-up bits of
paper dropped on a board and stuck where they fall,
or dense masses of mangled wire. The work of the
composer John Cage is rather typical of this tendency.
In the name of Zen, he has forsaken his earlier and
promising work with the "prepared piano," to confront
audiences with eight Ampex tape recorders simultaneously bellowing forth random noises. Or he has presented silent piano recitals where the performer has a
score consisting of nothing but rests, plus an assistant
to turn the pages, to jolt the audience into becoming
aware of the multiplicity of sounds that fill the musical
void—the shifting of feet and rustling of programs, the
titters of embarrassment, the coughing, and the rumble
of traffic outside.

There is, indeed, a considerable therapeutic value in
allowing oneself to be deeply aware of any sight or
sound that may arise. For one thing, it brings to mind
the marvel of seeing and hearing as such. For another,

the profound willingness to listen to or gaze upon anything at all frees the mind from fixed preconceptions of
beauty, creating, as it were, a free space in which altogether new forms and relationships may emerge. But
this is therapy; it is not yet art. It is on the level of the
random ramblings of a patient on the analyst's couch:
very important indeed as therapy, though it is by no
means the aim of psychoanalysis to substitute such
ramblings for conversation and literature. Cage's work
would be redeemed if he framed and presented it as a
kind of group session in audiotherapy, but as a concert
it is simply absurd. One may hope, however, that *after*
Cage has, by such listening, set his own mind free from
the composer's almost inevitable plagiarism of the forms
of the past, he will present us with the new musical patterns and relationships which he has not yet uttered.

Just as the skilled photographer often amazes us with
his lighting and framing of the most unlikely subjects,
so there are painters and writers in the West, as well
as in modern Japan, who have mastered the authenti-
cally Zen art of controlling accidents. Historically this
first arose in the Far East in the appreciation of the
rough texture of brush-strokes in calligraphy and painting, and in the accidental running of the glaze on
bowls made for the tea ceremony. One of the classical
instances of this kind of thing came about through the
shattering of a fine ceramic tea caddy, belonging to
one of the old Japanese tea masters. The fragments were
cemented together with gold, and its owner was amazed

at the way in which the random network of thin gold lines enhanced its beauty. It must be remembered, however, that this was an *objet trouvé*—an accidental effect *selected* by a man of exquisite taste, and treasured as one might treasure and exhibit a marvellous rock or a piece of driftwood. For in the Zen-inspired art of *bonseki*, or rock gardening, the stones are selected with infinite care, and though the hand of man may never have changed them it is far from true that any old stone will do. Furthermore, in calligraphy, painting, and ceramics, the accidental effects of running glaze or of flying hair-lines of the brush were accepted and presented by the artist only when he felt them to be fortuitous and unexpected marvels within the context of the work as a whole.

What governed his judgment? What gives *certain* accidental effects in painting the same beauty as the accidental outlines of clouds? According to Zen feeling there is no precise rule, no rule, that is to say, which can be formulated in words and taught systematically. On the other hand, there is in all these things a principle of order which in Chinese philosophy is termed *li*, and which Joseph Needham has translated "organic pattern." *Li* originally meant the markings in jade, the grain in wood, and the fiber in muscle. It designates a type of order which is too multidimensional, too subtly interrelated, and too squirmingly vital to be represented in words or mechanical images. The artist has to know it as he knows how to grow his hair. He can do it again and again, but can never explain how. In Taoist philosophy this power is called *te*, or "magical virtue." It is the element of the miraculous which we feel both at the stars in heaven and at our own ability to be conscious.

It is the possession of *te*, then, which makes all the difference between mere scrawls and the "white writing" of Mark Tobey, which admittedly derived its inspiration from Chinese calligraphy, or the multidimensional spontaneities of Gordon Onslow-Ford, who is, by the way, a considerable master of formal Chinese writing. It is by no means a purely haphazard drooling of paint or uncontrolled wandering of the brush, for the character and taste of such artists is visible in the grace (a possible equivalent of *te*) with which their strokes are formed even when they are not trying to represent anything except strokes. It is also what makes the difference between mere patches, smudges, and trails of black ink and the work of such Japanese moderns as Sabro Hasegawa and Onchi, which is after all in the *haboku* or "rough style" tradition of Sesshu. Anyone can write absolutely illegible Japanese, but who so enchantingly as Ryokwan? If it is true that "when the wrong man uses the right means, the right means work in the wrong way," it is often also true that when the right man uses the wrong means, the wrong means work in the right way.

The real genius of Chinese and Japanese Zen artists in their use of controlled accidents goes beyond the discovery of fortuitous beauty. It lies in being able to express, at the level of artistry, the realization of that ultimate standpoint from which "anything goes" and at which "all things are of one suchness." The mere selection of any random shape to stick in a frame simply confuses the metaphysical and the artistic domains; it does not express the one in terms of the other. Set in a frame, any old mess is at once cut off from the totality of its natural context, and for this very reason its manifestation of the Tao is concealed. The formless murmur of night noises in a great city has an enchantment which immediately disappears when formally presented as music in a concert hall. A frame outlines a universe, a microcosm, and if the contents of the frame are to rank as art they must have the same quality of relationship to the whole and to each other as events in the great universe, the macrocosm of nature. In nature the accidental is always recognized in relation to what is ordered and controlled. The dark *yin* is never without the bright *yang*. Thus the painting of Sesshu, the calligraphy of Ryokwan, and the ceramic bowls of the Hagi and Karatsu schools reveal the wonder of accidents in nature through accidents in a context of highly disciplined art.

The realization of the unswerving "rightness" of whatever happens is no more manifested by utter lawlessness in social conduct than by sheer caprice in art. As Zen has been used as a pretext for the latter in our times, its use as a pretext for the former is ancient history. Many a rogue has justified himself with the Buddhist formula, "Birth-and-death (*samsara*) is Nirvana; worldly passions are Enlightenment." This danger is implicit in Zen because it is implicit in freedom. Power and freedom can never be safe. They are dangerous in the same way that fire and electricity are dangerous. But it is quite pitiful to see Zen used as a pretext for license when the Zen in question is no more than an idea in the head, a simple rationalization. To some extent "Zen" is so used in the underworld which often attaches itself to artistic and intellectual communities. After all, the Bohemian way of life is primarily the natural consequence of artists and writers being so absorbed in their work that they have no interest in keeping up with the Joneses. It is also a symptom of creative changes in manners and morals which at first seem as reprehensible to conservatives as new forms in art. But every such community attracts a number of weak imitators and hangers-on, especially in the great cities, and it is mostly in this class that one now finds the stereotype of the "beatnik" with his phony Zen. Yet if Zen were not the pretext for this shiftless existence, it would be something else.

Is it, then, this underworld which is described in Kerouac's *Dharma Bums*? It is generally known that *The Dharma Bums* is not a novel but a flimsily fictionized account of the author's experiences in California in 1956. To anyone who knows the milieu described, the identity of each character is plain and it is no secret that Japhy Ryder, the hero of the story, is Gary Snyder.[1] Whatever may be said of Kerouac himself and of a few other characters in the story, it would be difficult indeed to fit Snyder into any stereotype of the Bohemian underworld. He has spent a year of Zen study in Kyoto, and has recently (1959) returned for another session, perhaps for two years this time. He is also a serious student of Chinese, having studied with Shih-hsiang Chen at the University of California, and superbly translated a number of the poems of the Zen hermit Han-shan.[2] His own work, scattered through many periodicals, entitles him to be regarded as one of the finest poets of the San Francisco renaissance.

But Snyder is, in the best sense, a bum. His manner of life is a quietly individualistic deviation from everything expected of a "good consumer." His temporary home is a little shack without utilities on a hillside in Mill Valley, at the top of a steep trail. When he needs money he goes to sea, or works as a firewatcher or logger. Otherwise, he stays at home or goes mountain climbing, most of the time writing, studying, or practicing Zen meditation. Part of his shack is set aside as a formal "meditation hall," and the whole place is in the

[1] The names were changed at the last minute, and at one point "Gary" remains instead of "Japhy." The excerpt published in the Summer, 1958, *Chicago Review* under the title "Meditation in the Woods" keeps the original names.

[2] "Cold Mountain Poems," *Evergreen Review,* vol. 2, no. 6, 1958.

best Zen tradition of clean and uncluttered simplicity. But this is not a Christian or Hinayana Buddhist style of asceticism. As *The Dharma Bums* made plain, it combines a voluntary and rather joyous poverty with a rich love-life, and for Western, and much Eastern, religiosity this is the touchstone of deviltry. This is not the place to argue the complex problem of spirituality and sexuality,[3] but one can only say, "So much the worse for such religiosity." This attitude has seldom been a part of Zen, new or old, beat or square.

In *The Dharma Bums*, however, we are seeing Snyder through Kerouac's eyes, and some distortions arise because Kerouac's own Buddhism is a true beat Zen which confuses "anything goes" at the existential level with "anything goes" on the artistic and social levels. Nevertheless, there is something endearing about Kerouac's personality as a writer, something which comes out in the warmth of his admiration for Gary, and in the lusty, generous enthusiasm for life which wells up at every point in his colorful and undisciplined prose. This exuberant warmth makes it impossible to put Kerouac in the class of the beat mentality described by John Clelland-Holmes—the cool, fake-intellectual hipster searching for kicks, name-dropping bits of Zen and jazz jargon to justify a disaffiliation from society which is in fact just ordinary, callous exploitation of other people. In the North Beach, Greenwich Village, and elsewhere

[3] For which see Part II of my *Nature, Man, and Woman*. New York, 1958.

such characters may occasionally be found, but no one has ever heard of any of them, and their identification with the active artists and poets of these communities is pure journalistic imagination. They are, however, the shadow of a substance, the low-level caricature which always attends spiritual and cultural movements, carrying them to extremes which their authors never intended. To this extent beat Zen is sowing confusion in idealizing as art and life what is better kept to oneself as therapy.

One of the most problematic characteristics of beat Zen, shared to some extent both by the creative artists and by their imitators, is the fascination of marijuana and peyote. That many of these people "take drugs" naturally lays them wide open to the most extreme forms of righteous indignation, despite the fact that marijuana and peyote (or its synthetic derivative, mescaline) are far less harmful and habit-forming than whiskey or tobacco. In these circles the smoking of marijuana is to some extent a sacramental point of honor, a religious defiance of square authority, equivalent to the refusal of the early Christians to burn incense to the Roman gods. Conversely, it is a matter of symbolic principle, as distinct from the enforcement of rational law, for the police to condemn marijuana, and sensational arrests of those who use it always provide a convenient diversion of public attention from serious crimes that continue to be overlooked.

The claim that these substances induce states of

consciousness equivalent to *satori* or mystical experience must be treated with some reserve. They certainly do not do so automatically, and some of their effects are quite unlike anything found in genuine mysticism. However, it is certainly true that for some people, perhaps with the requisite gift or ability, peyote, mescaline, or lysergic acid induces states which are distinctly favorable to mystical experience. As to marijuana, I have my doubts, though it appears to reduce the speed of subjective time.[4]

Now the underlying protestant lawlessness of beat Zen disturbs the square Zennists very seriously. For square Zen is the Zen of established tradition in Japan with its clearly defined hierarchy, its rigid discipline, and its specific tests of *satori*. More particularly, it is the kind of Zen adopted by Westerners studying in Japan, who will before long be bringing it back home. But there is an obvious difference between square Zen and the common or garden squareness of the Rotary Club or the Presbyterian Church. It is infinitely more imaginative, sensitive, and interesting. But it is still square because it is a quest for the *right* spiritual experience, for a *satori* which will receive the stamp

[4] As a result of experiments with lysergic acid conducted since the original version of this essay was written, I have been compelled to change the opinion then expressed as to the complete dissimilarity between some of these states of consciousness and mystical experience. The problem is discussed at length in the final essay in this volume, "The New Alchemy."

(*inka*) of approval and established authority. There will even be certificates to hang on the wall.

If square Zen falls into any serious excess it is in the direction of spiritual snobbism and artistic preciousness, though I have never known an orthodox Zen teacher who could be accused of either. These gentlemen seem to take their exalted office rather lightly, respecting its dignity without standing on it. The faults of square Zen are the faults of any spiritual in-group with an esoteric discipline and degrees of initiation. Students in the lower ranks can get unpleasantly uppity about inside knowledge which they are not at liberty to divulge—"and you wouldn't understand even if I could tell you"—and are apt to dwell rather sickeningly on the immense difficulties and iron disciplines of their task. There are times, however, when this is understandable, especially when someone who is just goofing off claims that he is following the Zen ideal of "naturalness."

The student of square Zen is also inclined at times to be niggling in his recognition of parallels to Zen in other spiritual traditions. Because the essentials of Zen can never be accurately and fully formulated, being an experience and not a set of ideas, it is always possible to be critical of anything anyone says about it, neither putting up nor shutting up. Any statement about Zen, or about spiritual experience of any kind, will always leave some aspect, some subtlety, unexpressed. No one's mouth is big enough to utter the whole thing. The

Western follower of Zen should also resist the temptation to associate himself with an even worse form of snobbery, the intellectual snobbery so largely characteristic of Far Eastern studies in American universities. In this particular field the fad for making humanistic studies "scientific" has gone to such wild extremes that even Suzuki is accused of being a "popularizer" instead of a serious scholar—presumably because he is a little unsystematic about footnotes and covers a vast area instead of confining himself with rigor to a single problem, e.g., "An Analysis of Some Illegible and Archaic Character-forms in the Tun-huang Manuscript of the Sutra of the Sixth Patriarch." There is a proper and honorable place in scholarship for the meticulous drudge, but when he is on top instead of on tap his dangerous envy of real intelligence drives all creative scholars from the field.[5]

In its artistic expression square Zen is often rather tediously studied and precious, a fate which all too easily befalls a venerable aesthetic tradition when its techniques are so highly developed that it takes a lifetime to master any one of them. No one has then the time to go beyond the achievements of the old masters,

[5] Suzuki, incidentally, is a very rare bird among contemporary Asians —an original thinker. He is no mere mouthpiece for any fixed tradition, and has come forth with some ideas about comparative religion and the psychology of religion which are of enormous importance, quite aside from what he has done to translate and interpret the literature of Zen. But it is just for this reason that people in square Zen, and academic Sinology have their qualms about accepting him.

so that new generations are condemned to endless repetition and imitation of their refinements. The student of *sumi* painting, calligraphy, *haiku* poetry, or tea ceremony can therefore get trapped in a tiresomely repetitious affectation of styles, varied only with increasingly esoteric allusions to the work of the past. When this comes to the point of imitating the old masters' happy accidents in such a way that "primitive" and "rough" effects are produced by the utmost practice and deliberation, the whole thing becomes so painful that even the wildest excesses of beat Zen art look refreshing. Indeed, it is possible that beat Zen and square Zen will so complement and rub against one another that an amazingly pure and lively Zen will arise from the hassle.

For this reason I see no really serious quarrel with either extreme. There was never a spiritual movement without its excesses and distortions. The experience of awakening which truly constitutes Zen is too timeless and universal to be injured. The extremes of beat Zen need alarm no one since, as Blake said, "the fool who persists in his folly will become wise." As for square Zen, "authoritative" spiritual experiences have always had a way of wearing thin, and thus of generating the demand for something genuine and unique which needs no stamp.

I have known followers of both extremes to come up with perfectly clear *satori* experiences, for since there is no real "way" to *satori* the way you are following makes very little difference.

But the quarrel *between* the extremes is of great philosophical interest, being a contemporary form of the ancient dispute between salvation by works and salvation by faith, or between what the Hindus called the ways of the monkey and of the cat. The cat—appropriately enough—follows the effortless way, since the mother cat carries her kittens. The monkey follows the hard way, since the baby monkey has to hang on to its mother's hair. Thus for beat Zen there must be no effort, no discipline, no artificial striving to attain *satori* or to be anything but what one is. But for square Zen there can be no true *satori* without years of meditation-practice under the stern supervision of a qualified master. In seventeenth-century Japan these two attitudes were *approximately* typified by the great masters Bankei and Hakuin, and it so happens that the followers of the latter "won out" and determined the present-day character of Rinzai Zen.[6]

Satori can lie along both roads. It is the concomitant of a "nongrasping" attitude of the senses to experience, and grasping can be exhausted by the discipline of directing its utmost intensity to a single, ever-elusive objective. But what makes the way of effort and will

[6] Rinzai Zen is the form most widely known in the West. There is also Soto Zen, which differs somewhat in technique, but is still closer to Hakuin than to Bankei. However, Bankei should not exactly be identified with beat Zen as I have described it, for he was certainly no advocate of the life of undisciplined whimsy despite all that he said about the importance of the uncalculated life and the folly of seeking *satori*.

power suspect to many Westerners is not so much an inherent laziness as a thorough familiarity with the wisdom of our own culture. The square Western Zennists are often quite naïve when it comes to an understanding of Christian theology or of all that has been discovered in modern psychiatry, for both have long been concerned with the fallibility and unconscious ambivalence of the will. Both have posed problems as to the vicious circle of seeking self-surrender or of "free-associating on purpose" or of accepting one's conflicts to escape from them, and to anyone who knows anything about either Christianity or psychotherapy these are very real problems. The interest of Chinese Zen and of people like Bankei is that they deal with these problems in a most direct and stimulating way, and begin to suggest some answers. But when Herrigel's Japanese archery master was asked, "How can I give up purpose on purpose?" he replied that no one had ever asked him that before. He had no answer except to go on trying blindly, for five years.

Foreign religions can be immensely attractive and highly overrated by those who know little of their own, and especially by those who have not worked through and grown out of their own. This is why the displaced or unconscious Christian can so easily use either beat or square Zen to justify himself. The one wants a philosophy to justify him in doing what he pleases. The other wants a more plausible authoritative salvation than the Church or the psychiatrists seem to be able to provide.

Furthermore the atmosphere of Japanese Zen is free from all one's unpleasant childhood associations with God the Father and Jesus Christ—though I know many young Japanese who feel just the same way about their early training in Buddhism. But the true character of Zen remains almost incomprehensible to those who have not surpassed the immaturity of needing to be justified, whether before the Lord God or before a paternalistic society.

The old Chinese Zen masters were steeped in Taoism. They saw nature in its total interrelatedness, and saw that every creature and every experience is in accord with the Tao of nature just as it is. This enabled them to accept themselves as they were, moment by moment, without the least need to justify anything. They didn't do it to defend themselves or to find an excuse for getting away with murder. They didn't brag about it and set themselves apart as rather special. On the contrary, their Zen was *wu-shih*, which means approximately "nothing special" or "no fuss." But Zen is "fuss" when it is mixed up with Bohemian affectations, and "fuss" when it is imagined that the only proper way to find it is to run off to a monastery in Japan or to do special exercises in the lotus posture for five hours a day. And I will admit that the very hullabaloo about Zen, even in such an essay as this, is also fuss—but a little less so.

Having said that, I would like to say something for all Zen fussers, beat or square. Fuss is all right, too. If you are hung on Zen, there's no need to try to pretend that you are not. If you really want to spend some years in a Japanese monastery, there is no earthly reason why you shouldn't. Or if you want to spend your me hopping freight cars and digging Charlie Parker, it's a free country.

> In the landscape of Spring there is neither better
>   nor worse;
> The flowering branches grow naturally, some long,
>   some short.

5

SPIRITUALITY AND SENSUALITY

Ir has often been said that the human being is a combination of angel and animal, a spirit imprisoned in flesh, a descent of divinity into materiality, charged with the duty of transforming the gross elements of the lower world into the image of God. Ordinarily this has been taken to mean that the animal and fleshly aspect of man is to be changed out of all recognition. Religious ideals of both East and West have envisaged the transformed human animal as something which has surpassed almost every aspect of the material body except perhaps shape, projecting the perfected man as a humanoid form without sensitivity to pain or passion, shrivelled and inert in sexuality, free from death and corruption, immune to disease, and even without weight or solidity. At least, something of this kind appears to be the nature of the resurrected and spiritualized body in traditional Christianity, foreshadowed already in the miraculous lives of the saints. Something of the same kind seems in certain forms of Hinduism to be expected of the *jivan-mukta*, the fully accomplished yogi delivered from material limitations while still manifesting his existence in the world.

It is possible that this is also the physical ideal of our own technological civilization, with its fixed intent of overcoming the limitations of time and space. Skeptical as we may be of achieving such material miracles by the power of prayer, meditation, and sanctity, we are perhaps some distance on the way to attaining them by medical and psychological techniques, bolstered by all the other powers of science. For we seem to look forward as ever to the total subjugation of hard and heavy substance to the airy rapidity of thought, and to the instant obedience of our weak and tender flesh to the bodiless flight of imagination. If science-fiction is any anticipation of the general direction of science, if the scientist here discloses (perhaps under a pseudonym) his secret intentions and dreams, it is obvious that technological man will not be content with exploring the universe at the insufferable crawl of the speed of light. His machines must eventually respond to the infinitely faster speed of thought if we are ever to get much farther out in space than our solar system, not to mention our single little galaxy.

Over against these spiritual and cerebral dreamers there are, and always have been, unashamedly earthbound souls who deplore this discontent with materiality. One thinks of the perennial pagan, the delightfully animal human who is not ashamed of his body, the sort of person who—at least in his healthier moments—is the natural conservative, the person who wants to say "Yes" to the physical world with all its limitations of time and mortality, space and distance, weight and solidity.

For centuries these two human types have been at war with each other, and one is constantly being pressed—so as to avoid mere mediocrity—to commit oneself to one side or the other, since "he who is not with us is against us, and whosoever does not gather with us scatters." We seem to like our human types to be black or white, and to despise the kind of person who cannot make up his mind between what seem to be absolutely demanding alternatives, but who vacillates indecisively, now to the ideals of spirit and now to the seductions of matter. Presumably this is just what the average and ordinary human being does. Neither the angel in him nor the animal in him can be repressed, and the strength of the two is so evenly balanced that they tend to cancel one another out to produce the common or garden mugwump, who, as the saying goes, has his mug on one side of the fence and his wump on the other. In the presence of those who have thoroughly committed themselves the average mugwump feels uncomfortable and vaguely guilty. Indecision is such an obvious and easily deplored weakness, such a sure butt for contempt by saint and satanist alike. So the poor mugwump simultaneously admires and is horrified by those who seem to have the strength of will to go one way or the other—those who decide to stand at all costs by the domineering and rational spirit, and those who abandon themselves with glee to the intense pleasure-pain of sensuality.

Especially deplorable is the kind of person who might be called the extreme mugwump—the one who has his extremities very far out on both sides of the fence. There is, for example, the common scandal of the saint-sinner, the individual who appears in public as the champion of the spirit, but who is in private some sort of rake. Very often his case is not so simple as that of the mere hypocrite. He is genuinely attracted to both extremes. Not only does social convention compel him to publish one and suppress the other, but most often he is himself horribly torn between the two. He veers between moods of intense holiness and of outrageous licentiousness, suffering between times the most appalling pangs of conscience. The type is, indeed, especially common in clerical and academic circles, just because these vocations attract highly sensitive human beings who feel the lure of both extremes more strongly than others. Only in the artist is this duplicity more or less accepted, perhaps because beauty is the one attribute shared in common by God and the Devil, because devotion to the beautiful, as distinct from the good and the true, seems to make one a human being who is not altogether serious—neither man nor devil but some kind of elf, consigned in the Day of Judgment neither to heaven nor to hell but to the limbo of souls without moral sense. It is thus that for our society the artist is a kind of harmless clown, an entertainer from whom nothing is expected save proficiency in the realm of the irrelevant, since his function is taken to be no more than the decoration of surfaces. For this reason the artist can get away with a private life that would be scandalous for the priest or the professor.

Now all of this raises the question as to whether the proper outcome of man's dual nature ought to be a victory for one side or the other. Catholic theology, for example, stands at least in theory for a marriage of the spirit and the flesh, for, as St. Thomas Aquinas held, divine grace does not obliterate nature but perfects it. But in practice the perfection of nature has always meant its total submission to the spirit, and it is only quite recently that Catholic Christians like Eric Gill and G. K. Chesterton have been able to carry off a rollicking spiritual materialism. This made them excellent decoys for prospective converts, but note that one was an artist and the other a writer, and neither is in danger of being canonized. For the fact remains that traditional Christianity will put up with the flesh only so long as its demands are extremely moderate and demure, just so long as the cloven hoof of Pan never puts in an appearance. One suspects that this gesture toward nature and materiality is the same sort of "come-on" as the regular-guy priest, admired out of all proportion for little human traits that would be unnoticed in a layman.

It is high time to ask whether it is really any scandal, any deplorable inconsistency, for a human being to be both angel and animal with equal devotion. Is it not possible, in other words, to be the extreme mugwump without inner conflict, to be mystic and sensualist without actual contradiction? It is hard to see how a human being can be anything but a mediocrity on the one hand or a fanatic on the other unless he can give rein to both sides of his nature, avoiding, however, the deceit and degradation which attach themselves to the animal side of our life when it is associated with shame. The philosophy of the out-and-out pagan, the romanticist of nature and the flesh, is by itself enormously superficial—lacking in wonder at disease and death, which are quite as normal as good health, and deficient in that combination of awe and curiosity which urges on the mystic to marvel at the overwhelmingly odd fact of simple is-ness, to stretch his imagination to the furthest limits of time and space, and to explore the inward mystery of his own consciousness. The logical grammarian's opinion that such inquiries are simply meaningless appears to be nothing more than a new variation on the old psychological type that gets the words but never understands the music. On the other hand, the mystic who has no part in the earthiness and allure of nature is sterile rather than pure, an extreme type of cerebrotonic ectomorph, i.e., skinny abstractionist, who lives in a world of ideas without concrete meanings. Furthermore, the philosophy of the pure spiritist, even when he allows that God created nature, can never explain how the good Lord so forgot himself as to make anything so allegedly impure.

It has often been noted that mysticism expresses itself in the language of natural love and that mystics of the Christian tradition have made particular use of the Bible's great love poem, the *Song of Songs*. Psychologists with a slant to materialism therefore argue that mysticism is nothing but sublimated sexuality and frustrated fleshliness, whereas the spiritists maintain that the love-imagery is nothing but allegory and symbolism never to be taken in its gross and animal sense. But is it not possible that both parties are right and wrong, and that the love of nature and the love of spirit are paths upon a circle which meet at their extremes? Perhaps the meeting is discovered only by those who follow both at once. Such a course seems impossible and inconsistent only if it can be held that love is a matter of choosing between alternatives, if, in other words, love is an exclusive attitude of mind which cleaves to one object and rejects all others. If so, it must be quite other than what is said to be God's own love, "who maketh his sun to shine upon the evil and the good, and sendeth his rain upon the just and the unjust." Love is surely a disposition of the heart which radiates on all sides like light. At the same time, love may choose one object rather than others, not because that object is innately and absolutely preferable, but because the limitations of human energy require concentration for depth of experience. Polygamy, for example, would be all very well if one had unlimited time to devote to each spouse.

But are God and nature, spirit and flesh—like individual persons—mutually exclusive? "He that is unmarried," said St. Paul, "careth for the things that belong to the Lord, how he may please the Lord. But he that is married careth for the things that are of the world, how he may please his wife." Yet this is to say that the divine cannot be loved in and through the things of this world, and to deny the saying that "Inasmuch as you have done it unto one of the least of these my brethren, you have done in unto me." If the love of God and the love of the world are mutually exclusive, then, on the very premises of theology, God is a finite thing among things —for only finite things exclude one another. God is dethroned and un-godded by being put in opposition to nature and the world, becoming an object instead of the continuum in which we "live and move and have our being."

Not to cherish both the angel and the animal, both the spirit and the flesh, is to renounce the whole interest and greatness of being human, and it is really tragic that those in whom the two natures are equally strong should be made to feel in conflict with themselves. For the saint-sinner and the mystic-sensualist is always the most interesting type of human being because he is the most complete. When the two aspects are seen to be consistent with each other, there is a real sense in which spirit transforms nature: that is to say, the animality of the mystic is always richer, more refined, and more subtly sensuous than the animality of the merely animal man. For to say that man is both god and devil is *not* to say that spiritually minded people should spend some of their time robbing banks and torturing children. Such violent excesses of passion are bred from the frustration of pursuing either aspect of our nature to the exclusion of the other. They arise when the ruthless idealism of the spirit is unhumanized by the weakness of the flesh, or when the blind desire of the flesh is unenlightened by the wisdom of the spirit—which knows that the exclusive pursuit of pleasure is as frustrating and absurd as the old quest for perpetual motion. The violent, ultrasatanic devil in man is either the repressed Christ or the repressed Pan, the right and the left hands of God, who said to the prophet Isaiah, "I am the Lord, and there is none else. I form the light, and create darkness; I make peace, and create evil; I the Lord do all these things."

We noted that our society tolerates the full life, the love of both spirit and nature, only in the artist, but just because it does not take him seriously, because it regards him as an entertaining irrelevance. The man of deep spiritual wisdom is also irrelevant to this society, whether entertaining or otherwise. This has not just recently come to be so; it has been so for centuries, because—for centuries—society has consisted precisely of those human beings who are so deluded by the conventions of words and ideas as to believe that there is a real choice between the great opposites of life—between pleasure and pain, good and evil, God and Lucifer, spirit and nature. But what is separable in terms, in words, is not separable in reality—in the solid relationship between the terms. Whoever sees that there is no ultimate choice between these opposites is irrelevant because he cannot really participate in the politician's and the ad-man's illusion that there can be better and better without worse and worse, and that matter can yield indefinitely to the desires of mind without becoming utterly undesirable. It is not so much that there are fixed limits to our skill and technological power as that there are limits to our own perception: that we cannot see the figure without the background, the solid without the space, motion without time, action without resistance, joy without sorrow.

We have only to imagine what would happen if thought and spirit had their way without hindrance, with God's supposed omnipotence to have every wish granted instantaneously. Nothing would any longer be worth wishing for. There is an old fairy tale of a fisherman who once caught a marvellous golden fish. For the fish spoke, promising him that if he would return it to the water he would be granted three wishes. Having released the fish, he went home to his wife to talk over what the wishes should be, on the assurance that the fish would be waiting for him at the same place the following day. The old lady sent him back with the request that their broken-down cottage be transformed into a mansion with servants and spacious lands. That night, the fisherman came home to find that all had happened as requested. But in the course of only a few days the rapacious wife was hankering to be an archduchess with a vast palace equipped with guards and retainers, with terraces and formal gardens, situated in the midst of a great feudal domain. And again the wish was granted. Yet with one wish remaining the wife's greed increased and increased so that she made up her mind to wish for all that could be wished—to be ruler of the sun and moon and stars, of the earth and mountains and oceans, of all birds in the air, fishes in the sea, and of all men in the world. But when the fisherman repeated her desire to the golden fish it replied, "Such a wish is not mine to grant, and, for her arrogance, she shall be returned to the state from which she started." Returning that night, the fisherman found once again the broken-down cottage, and his wife again in rags. And yet, in a way, her wish was granted.

6

THE NEW ALCHEMY

Besides the philosopher's stone that would turn base metal into gold, one of the great quests of alchemy in both Europe and Asia was the elixir of immortality. In gullible enthusiasm for this quest, more than one Chinese emperor died of the fabulous concoctions of powdered jade, tea, ginseng, and precious metals prepared by Taoist priests. But just as the work of transforming lead into gold was in many cases a chemical symbolism for a spiritual transformation of man himself, so the immortality to be conferred by the elixir was not always the literally everlasting life but rather the transportation of consciousness into a state beyond time. Modern physicists have solved the problem of changing lead into gold, though the process is somewhat more expensive than digging gold from the earth. But in the last few years modern chemists have prepared one or two substances for which it may be claimed that in some cases they induce states of mind remarkably similar to cosmic consciousness.

To many people such claims are deeply disturbing. For one thing, mystical experience seems altogether too easy when it simply comes out of a bottle, and is thus available to people who have done nothing to deserve it, who have neither fasted nor prayed nor practiced yoga. For another, the claim seems to imply that spiritual insight is after all only a matter of body chemistry involving a total reduction of the spiritual to the material. These are serious considerations, even though one may be convinced that in the long run the difficulty is found to rest upon semantic confusion as to the definitions of "spiritual" and "material."

However, it should be pointed out that there is nothing new or disreputable in the idea that spiritual insight is an undeserved gift of divine grace, often conveyed through such material or sacramental means as the water of baptism and the bread and wine of the mass. The priest who by virtue of his office transforms bread and wine into the body and blood of Christ, *ex opere operato*, by the simple repetition of the formula of the Last Supper, is in a situation not radically different from that of the scientist who, by repeating the right formula of an experiment, may effect a transformation in the brain. The comparative worth of the two operations must be judged by their effects. There were always those upon whom the sacraments of baptism and communion did not seem to "take," whose lives remained effectively unregenerate. Likewise, none of these consciousness-changing chemicals are literally mystical experience in a bottle. Many who receive them experience only ecstasies without insight, or just an unpleasant confusion of sensation and imagination. States akin to mystical experience arise only in certain individuals and then often depend upon considerable concentration and effort to use the change of consciousness in certain ways. It is important here, too, to stress the point that ecstasy is only incidental to the authentic mystical experience, the essence of which might best be described as insight, as the word is now used in psychiatry.

A chemical of this kind might perhaps be said to be an aid to perception in the same way as the telescope, microscope, or spectroscope, save in this case that the instrument is not an external object but an internal state of the nervous system. All such instruments are relatively useless without proper training and preparation not only in their handling, but also in the particular field of investigation.

These considerations alone are already almost enough to show that the use of such chemicals does not reduce spiritual insight to a mere matter of body chemistry. But it should be added that even when we can describe certain events in terms of chemistry this does not mean that such events are merely chemical. A chemical description of spiritual experience has somewhat the same use and the same limits as the chemical description of a great painting. It is simple enough to make a chemical analysis of the paint, and for artists and connoisseurs alike there is some point in doing so. It might also be possible to work out a chemical description of all the processes that go on in the artist while he is painting. But it would be incredibly complicated, and in the meantime the same processes could be described and communicated far more effectively in some other language than the chemical. We should probably say that a process *is* chemical only when chemical language is the most effective means of describing it. Analogously, some of the chemicals known as psychodelics provide opportunities for mystical insight in much the same way that well-prepared paints and brushes provide opportunities for fine painting, or a beautifully constructed piano for great music. They make it easier, but they do not accomplish the work all by themselves.

The two chemicals which are of most use in creating a change of consciousness conducive to spiritual experience are mescaline and lysergic acid diethylamide (known, for short, as LSD). The former is a synthetic formulation of the active ingredients of the peyote cactus, and the latter a purely synthetic chemical of the indole group which produces its effects even in such minute amounts as twenty-five micrograms. The specific effects of these chemicals are hard to identify with any clarity, and so far as is known at present they seem to operate upon the nervous system by reducing some of the inhibitory mechanisms which ordinarily have a screening effect upon our consciousness. Certain psychiatrists who seem overly anxious to hang on to the socially approved sensation of reality—more or less the world as perceived on a bleak Monday morning—classify these chemicals as hallucinogens producing toxic effects of a schizoid or psychotic character. I am afraid this is psychiatric gobbledygook: a sort of authoritative rumble of disapproval. Neither substance is an addictive drug, like heroin or opium, and it has never been demonstrated that they have harmful effects upon people who were not otherwise seriously disturbed. It is begging the question to call the changes of consciousness which they educe hallucinations, for some of the unusual things felt and seen may be no more unreal than the unfamiliar forms perceived through a microscope. We do not know. It is also begging the question to call their effects toxic, which might mean poisonous, unless this word can also be used for the effects of vitamins or proteins. Such language is evaluative, not descriptive in any scientific sense.

Somewhat more than two years ago (1958) I was asked by a psychiatric research group to take 100 micrograms of lysergic acid, to see whether it would reproduce anything resembling a mystical experience. It did not do so, and so far as I know the reason was that I had not then learned how to direct my inquiries when under its influence. It seemed instead that my senses had been given a kaleidoscopic character (and this is no more than a metaphor) which made the whole world entrancingly complicated, as if I were involved in a multidimensional arabesque. Colors became so vivid that flowers, leaves, and fabrics seemed to be illumined from inside. The random patterns of blades of grass in a lawn appeared to be exquisitely organized without, however, any actual distortion of vision. Black ink or *sumi* paintings by Chinese and Japanese artists appeared almost to be three-dimensional photographs, and what are ordinarily dismissed as irrelevant details of speech, behavior, appearance, and form seemed in some indefinable way to be highly significant. Listening to music with closed eyes, I beheld the most fascinating patterns of dancing jewelry, mosaic, tracery, and abstract images. At one point everything appeared to be uproariously funny, especially the gestures and actions of people going about their everyday business. Ordinary remarks seemed to reverberate with double and quadruple meanings, and the role-playing behavior of those around me not only became unusually evident but also implied concealed attitudes contrary or complementary to its overt intention. In short, the screening or selective apparatus of our normal interpretative evaluation of experience had been partially suspended, with the result that I was presumably projecting the sensation of meaning or significance upon just about everything. The whole experience was vastly entertaining and interesting, but as yet nothing like any mystical experience that I had had before.

It was not until a year later that I tried LSD again, this time at the request of another research team. Since then I have repeated the experiment five times, with dosages varying from 75 to 100 micrograms. My impression has been that such experiments are profound and rewarding to the extent that I do my utmost to observe perceptual and evaluative changes and to describe them as clearly and completely as possible, usually with the help of a tape recorder. To give a play-by-play description of each experiment might be clinically interesting, but what I am concerned with here is a philosophical discussion of some of the high points and recurrent themes of my experiences. Psychiatrists have not yet made up their minds as to whether LSD is useful in therapy, but at present I am strongly inclined to feel that its major use may turn out to be only secondarily as a therapeutic and primarily as an instrumental aid to the creative artist, thinker, or scientist. I should observe, in passing, that the human and natural environment in which these experiments are conducted is of great importance, and that its use in hospital wards with groups of doctors firing off clinical questions at the subject is most undesirable. The supervising physician should take a human attitude, and drop all defensive dramatizations of scientific objectivity and medical authority, conducting the experiment in surroundings of some natural or artistic beauty.

I have said that my general impression of the first experiment was that the "mechanism" by which we screen our sense-data and select only some of them as significant had been partially suspended. Consequently, I felt that the particular feeling which we associate with "the meaningful" was projected indiscriminately upon everything, and then rationalized in ways that might strike an independent observer as ridiculous—unless, perhaps, the subject were unusually clever at rationalizing. However, the philosopher cannot pass up the point that our selection of some sense-data as significant and others as insignificant is always with relation to particular purposes—survival, the quest for certain pleasures, finding one's way to some destination, or whatever it may be. But in every experiment with LSD one of the first effects I have noticed is a profound relaxation combined with an abandonment of purposes and goals, reminding me of the Taoist saying that "when purpose has been used to achieve purposelessness, the thing has been grasped." I have felt, in other words, endowed with all the time in the world, free to look about me as if I were living in eternity without a single problem to be solved. It is just for this reason that the busy and purposeful actions of other people seem at this time to be so comic, for it becomes obvious that by setting themselves goals which are always in the future, in the "tomorrow which never comes," they are missing entirely the point of being alive.

When, therefore, our selection of sense-impressions is not organized with respect to any particular purpose, all the surrounding details of the world must appear to be equally meaningful or equally meaningless. Logically, these are two ways of saying the same thing, but the overwhelming feeling of my own LSD experiences is that all aspects of the world become meaningful rather than meaningless. This is not to say that they acquire meaning in the sense of signs, by virtue of pointing to something else, but that all things appear to be their own point. Their simple existence, or better, their present formation, seems to be perfect, to be an end or fulfillment without any need for justification. Flowers do not bloom in order to produce seeds, nor are seeds germinated in order to bring forth flowers. Each stage of the process—seed, sprout, bud, flower, and fruit—may be regarded as the goal. A chicken is one egg's way of producing others. In our normal experience something of the same kind takes place in music and the dance, where the point of the action is each moment of its unfolding and not just the temporal end of the performance.

Such a translation of everyday experience into something of the same nature as music has been the beginning and the prevailing undertone of all my experiments. But LSD does not simply suspend the selective process by cutting it out. It would be more exact to say that it shows the relativity of our ordinary evaluation of sense-data by suggesting others. It permits the mind to organize its sensory impressions in new patterns. In my second experiment I noticed, for example, that all repeated forms—leaves on a stem, books on shelves, mullions in windows—gave me the sensation of seeing double or even multiple, as if the second, third, and fourth leaves on the stem were reflections of the first, seen, as it were, in several thicknesses of window glass. When I mentioned this, the attending physician held up his finger to see if it would give me a double image. For a moment it seemed to do so, but all at once I saw that the second image had its basis in a wisp of cigar smoke passing close to his finger and upon which my consciousness had projected the highlights and outline of a second finger. As I then concentrated upon this sensation of doubling or repeating images, it seemed suddenly as if the whole field of sight were a transparent liquid rippled in concentric circles as in dropping a stone into a pool. The normal images of things around me were not distorted by this pattern. They remained just as usual, but my attention directed itself to highlights, lines, and shadows upon them that fitted the pattern, letting those that did not fall into relative insignificance. As soon, however, as I noticed this projection and became aware of details that did not fit the pattern, it seemed as if whole handfuls of pebbles had been thrown into the optical space, rippling it with concentric circles that overlapped in all directions, so that every visible point became an intersection of circles. The optical field seemed, in fact, to have a structured grain like a photograph screened for reproduction, save that the organization of the grains was not rectilinear but circular. In this way every detail fitted the pattern and the field of vision became *pointillist*, like a painting by Seurat.

This sensation raised a number of questions. Was my mind imperiously projecting its own geometrical designs upon the world, thus "hallucinating" a structure in things which is not actually there? Or is what we call the "real" structure of things simply a learned projection or hallucination which we hold in common? Or was I somehow becoming aware of the actual grain of the rods and cones in my retina, for even a hallucination must have some actual basis in the nervous system? On another occasion I was looking closely at a handful of sand, and in becoming aware that I could not get it into clear focus I became conscious of every detail and articulation of the way in which my eyes were fuzzing the image—and this was certainly perception of a grain or distortion in the eyes themselves.

The general impression of these optical sensations is that the eyes, without losing the normal area of vision, have become microscopes, and that the texture of the visual field is infinitely rich and complex. I do not know whether this is actual awareness of the multiplicity of nerve-endings in the retina, or, for that matter, in the fingers, for the same grainy feeling arose in the sense of touch. But the effect of feeling that this is or may be so is, as it were, to turn the senses back upon themselves, and so to realize that seeing the external world is *also* seeing the eyes. In other words, I became vividly aware of the fact that what I call shapes, colors, and textures in the outside world are also states of my nervous system, that is, of me. In knowing them I also know myself. But the strange part of this apparent sensation of my own senses was that I did not appear to be inspecting them from outside or from a distance, as if they were *objects*. I can say only that the awareness of grain or structure in the senses seemed to be awareness of awareness, of myself from inside myself. Because of this, it followed that the distance or separation between myself and my senses, on the one hand, and the external world, on the other, seemed to disappear. I was no longer a detached observer, a little man inside my own head, *having* sensations. I was the sensations, so much so that there was nothing left of me, the observing ego, except the series of sensations which happened —not to me, but just happened—moment by moment, one after another.

To become the sensations, as distinct from having them, engenders the most astonishing sense of freedom and release. For it implies that experience is not something in which one is trapped or by which one is pushed around, or against which one must fight. The conventional duality of subject and object, knower and known, feeler and feeling, is changed into a polarity: the knower and the known become the poles, terms, or phases of a single event which happens, not *to* me or *from* me, but of itself. The experiencer and the experience become a single, ever-changing, self-forming process, complete and fulfilled at every moment of its unfolding, and of infinite complexity and subtlety. It is like, not watching, but being, a coiling arabesque of smoke patterns in the air, or of ink dropped in water, or of a dancing snake which seems to move from every part of its body at once. This may be a "drug-induced hallucination," but it corresponds exactly to what Dewey and Bentley have called the transactional relationship of the organism to its environment. This is to say that all our actions and experiences arise mutually from the organism and from the environment at the same time. The eyes can see light because of the sun, but the sun is light because of the eyes. Ordinarily, under the hypnosis of social conditioning, we feel quite distinct from our physical surroundings, facing them rather than belonging in them. Yet in this way we ignore and screen out the physical fact of our total interdependence with the natural world. We are as embodied in it as our own cells and molecules are embodied in us. Our neglect and repression of this interrelationship gives special urgency to all the new sciences of ecology, studying the interplay of organisms with their environments, and warning us against ignorant interference with the balances of nature.

The sensation that events are happening of themselves, and that nothing is *making* them happen and that they are not happening *to* anything, has always been a major feature of my experiences with LSD. It is possible that the chemical is simply giving me a vivid realization of my own philosophy, though there have been times when the experience has suggested modifications of my previous thinking.[1] But just as the sensation of subject-object polarity is confirmed by the transactional psychology of Dewey and Bentley, so the sensation of events happening "of themselves" is just how one would expect to perceive a world consisting entirely of process. Now the language of science is increasingly a language of process—a description of events, relations, operations, and forms rather than of things and substances. The world so described is a world of actions rather than agents, verbs rather than nouns, going against the common-sense idea that an action is the behavior of some *thing*, some solid entity of "stuff." But the common-sense idea that action is always the function of an agent is so deeply rooted, so bound up with our sense of order and security, that seeing the world to be otherwise can be seriously disturbing. Without agents, actions do not seem to come from anywhere, to have any dependable origin, and at first sight this spontaneity can be alarming. In one experiment it seemed that whenever I tried to put my (metaphorical) foot upon some solid ground,

[1] I have often made the point, as in *The Way of Zen*, that the "real" world is concrete rather than abstract, and thus that the conceptual patterns of order, categorization, and logic which the human mind projects upon nature are in some way less real. But upon several occasions LSD has suggested a fundamental identity of percept and concept, concrete and abstract. After all, our brains and the patterns in them are themselves members of the concrete, physical universe, and thus our abstractions are as much forms of nature as the structure of crystals or the organization of ferns.

the ground collapsed into empty space. I could find no substantial basis from which to act: my will was a whim, and my past, as a causal conditioning force, had simply vanished. There was only the present conformation of events, happening. For a while I felt lost in a void, frightened, baseless, insecure through and through. Yet soon I became accustomed to the feeling, strange as it was. There was simply a pattern of action, of process, and this was at one and the same time the universe and myself with nothing outside it either to trust or mistrust. And there seemed to be no meaning in the idea of its trusting or mistrusting itself, just as there is no possibility of a finger's touching its own tip.

Upon reflection, there seems to be nothing unreasonable in seeing the world in this way. The agent behind every action is itself action. If a mat can be called matting, a cat can be called catting. We do not actually need to ask who or what "cats," just as we do not need to ask what is the basic stuff or substance out of which the world is formed—for there is no way of describing this substance except in terms of form, of structure, order, and operation. The world is not *formed* as if it were inert clay responding to the touch of a potter's hand; the world *is* form, or better, formation, for upon examination every substance turns out to be closely knit pattern. The fixed notion that every pattern or form must be made of some basic material which is in itself formless is based on a superficial analogy between natural formation and manufacture, as if the stars and rocks had been made out of something as a carpenter makes tables out of wood. Thus what we call the agent behind the action is simply the prior or relatively more constant state of the same action: when a man runs we have a "manning-running" over and above a simple "manning." Furthermore, it is only a somewhat clumsy convenience to say that present events are moved or caused by past events, for we are actually talking about earlier and later stages of the same event. We can establish regularities of rhythm and pattern in the course of an event, and so predict its future configurations, but its past states do not "push" its present and future states as if they were a row of dominoes stood on end so that knocking over the first collapses all the others in series. The fallen dominoes lie where they fall, but past events vanish into the present, which is just another way of saying that the world is a self-moving pattern which, when its successive states are remembered, can be shown to have a certain order. Its motion, its energy, issues from itself now, not from the past, which simply falls behind it in memory like the wake from a ship.

When we ask the "why" of this moving pattern, we usually try to answer the question in terms of its original, past impulse or of its future goal. I had realized for a long time that if there is in any sense a reason for the world's existence it must be sought in the present, as the reason for the wake must be sought in the engine of the moving ship. I have already mentioned that LSD makes me peculiarly aware of the musical or dancelike character of the world, bringing my attention to rest upon its present flowing and seeing this as its ultimate point. Yet I have also been able to see that this point has depths, that the present wells up from within itself with an energy which is something much richer than simple exuberance.

One of these experiments was conducted late at night. Some five or six hours from its start the doctor had to go home, and I was left alone in the garden. For me, this stage of the experiment is always the most rewarding in terms of insight, after some of its more unusual and bizarre sensory effects have worn off. The garden was a lawn surrounded by shrubs and high trees —pine and eucalyptus—and floodlit from the house which enclosed it on one side. As I stood on the lawn I noticed that the rough patches where the grass was thin or mottled with weeds no longer seemed to be blemishes. Scattered at random as they were, they appeared to constitute an ordered design, giving the whole area the texture of velvet damask, the rough patches being the parts where the pile of the velvet is cut. In sheer delight I began to dance on this enchanted carpet, and through the thin soles of my moccasins I could feel the ground becoming alive under my feet, connecting me with the earth and the trees and the sky in such a way that I seemed to become one body with my whole surroundings.

Looking up, I saw that the stars were colored with the same reds, greens, and blues that one sees in iridescent glass, and passing across them was the single light of a jet plane taking forever to streak over the sky. At the same time, the trees, shrubs, and flowers seemed to be living jewelry, inwardly luminous like intricate structures of jade, alabaster, or coral, and yet breathing and flowing with the same life that was in me. Every plant became a kind of musical utterance, a play of variations on a theme repeated from the main branches, through the stalks and twigs, to the leaves, the veins in the leaves, and to the fine capillary network between the veins. Each new bursting of growth from a center repeated or amplified the basic design with increasing complexity and delight, finally exulting in a flower.

From my description it will seem that the garden acquired an atmosphere that was distinctly exotic, like the gardens of precious stones in the *Arabian Nights*, or like scenes in a Persian miniature. This struck me at the time, and I began to wonder just why it is that the glowingly articulated landscapes of those miniatures seem exotic, as do also many Chinese and Japanese paintings. Were the artists recording what they, too, had seen under the influence of drugs? I knew enough of the lives and techniques of Far Eastern painters to doubt this. I asked, too, whether what I was seeing was "drugged." In other words, was the effect of the LSD in my nervous system the addition to my senses of some chemical screen which distorted all that I saw to preternatural loveliness? Or was its effect rather to remove certain habitual and normal inhibitions of the mind and senses, enabling us to see things as they would appear to us if we were not so chronically repressed? Little is known of the exact neurological effects of LSD, but what is known suggests the latter possibility. If this be so, it is possible that the art forms of other cultures appear exotic—that is, unfamiliarly enchanting—because we are seeing the world through the eyes of artists whose repressions are not the same as ours. The blocks in their view of the world may not coincide with ours, so that in their representations of life we see areas that we normally ignore. I am inclined to some such solution because there have been times when I have seen the world in this magical aspect without benefit of LSD, and they were times when I was profoundly relaxed within, my senses unguardedly open to their surroundings.

Feeling, then, not that I was drugged but that I was in an unusual degree open to reality, I tried to discern the meaning, the inner character of the dancing pattern which constituted both myself and the garden, and the whole dome of the night with its colored stars. All at once it became obvious that the whole thing was love-play, where love means everything that the word can mean, a spectrum ranging from the red of erotic delight, through the green of human endearment, to the violet of divine charity, from Freud's libido to Dante's "love that moves the sun and other stars." All were so many colors issuing from a single white light, and, what was more, this single source was not just love as we ordinarily understand it: it was also intelligence, not only

Eros and Agape but also Logos. I could see that the intricate organization both of the plants and of my own nervous system, alike symphonies of branching complexity, were not just manifestations of intelligence—as if things like intelligence and love were in themselves substances or formless forces. It was rather that the pattern itself *is* intelligence and *is* love, and this somehow in spite of all its outwardly stupid and cruel distortions.

There is probably no way of finding objective verification for insights such as this. The world is love to him who treats it as such, even when it torments and destroys him, and in states of consciousness where there is no basic separation between the ego and the world suffering cannot be felt as malice inflicted upon oneself by another. By the same logic it might seem that without the separation of self and other there can be no love. This might be true if individuality and universality were formal opposites, mutually exclusive of one another, if, that is, the inseparability of self and other meant that all individual differentiations were simply unreal. But in the unitary, or nondualistic, view of the world I have been describing this is not so. Individual differences express the unity, as branches, leaves, and flowers from the same plant, and the love between the members is the realization of their basic interdependence.

I have not yet been able to use LSD in circumstances of great physical or moral pain, and therefore my explorations of the problem of evil under its influence may appear to be shallow. Only once in these experiments have I felt acute fear, but I know of several cases in which LSD has touched off psychic states of the most alarming and unpleasant kind. More than once I have invited such states under LSD by looking at images ordinarily suggestive of "the creeps"—the mandibles of spiders, and the barbs and spines of dangerous fish and insects. Yet they evoked only a sense of beauty and exuberance, for our normal projection of malice into these creatures was entirely withdrawn, so that their organs of destruction became no more evil than the teeth of a beautiful woman. On another occasion I looked for a long time at a colored reproduction of Van Eyck's *Last Judgment*, which is surely one of the most horrendous products of human imagination. The scene of hell is dominated by the figure of Death, a skeleton beneath whose batlike wings lies a writhing mass of screaming bodies gnawed by snakes which penetrate them like maggots in fruit. One of the curious effects of LSD is to impart an illusion of movement in still images, so that here the picture came to life and the whole entanglement of limbs and serpents began to squirm before my eyes.[2]

[2] Later, with the aid of a sea urchin's shell, I was able to find out something of the reasons for this effect. All the small purple protrusions on the shell seemed to be wiggling, not only to sight but also to touch. Watching this phenomenon closely, I realized that as my eyes moved across the shell they seemed to change the intensity of color-

Ordinarily such a sight should have been hideous, but now I watched it with intense and puzzled interest until the thought came to me, *"Demon est deus inversus* —the Devil is God inverted—so let's turn the picture upside down."* I did so, and thereupon burst into laughter for it became apparent at once that the scene was an empty drama, a sort of spiritual scarecrow, designed to guard some mystery from profanation by the ignorant. The agonized expressions of the damned seemed quite evidently "put on," and as for the death's-head, the great skull in the center of the painting, it became just what a skull is—an empty shell—and why the horror when there is nothing in it?

I was, of course, seeing ecclesiastical hells for what they are. On the one hand, they are the pretension that social authority is ultimately inescapable since there are post-mortem police who will catch every criminal. On the other hand, they are "no trespassing" signs to discourage the insincere and the immature from attaining insights which they might abuse. A baby is put in a play pen to keep it from getting at the matches or falling downstairs, and though the intention of the pen is to keep the baby closed in, parents are naturally proud

ing, amounting to an increase or decrease in the depth of shadow. This did not happen when the eyes were held still. Now motion, or apparent motion, of the shadow will often seem to be motion of the object casting it, in this case the protrusions on the shell. In the Van Eyck painting there was likewise an alteration, a lightening or darkening, of actual shadows which the artist had painted, and thus the same illusion of movement.

when the child grows strong enough to climb out. Likewise, a man can perform actions which are truly moral only when he is no longer motivated by the fear of hell, that is, when he grows into union with the Good that is beyond good and evil, which, in other words, does not act from the love of rewards or the fear of punishments. This is precisely the nature of the world when it is considered as self-moving action, giving out a past instead of being motivated by a past.

Beyond this, the perception of the empty threat of the death's-head was certainly a recognition of the fact that the fear of death, as distinct from the fear of dying, is one of the most baseless mirages that trouble us. Because it is completely impossible to imagine one's own personal absence, we fill the void in our minds with images of being buried alive in perpetual darkness. If death is the simple termination of a stream of consciousness, it is certainly nothing to fear. At the same time, I realize that there is some apparent evidence for survival of death in a few extraordinarily unexplainable mediumistic communications and remembrances of past lives. These I attribute, vaguely enough, to subtler networks of communication and interrelationship in the pattern of life than we ordinarily perceive. For if forms repeat themselves, if the structure of branching trees is reverberated in the design of watercourses in the desert, it would not be so strange if a pattern so intricate as the human nervous system were to repeat configurations that arise in consciousness as veritable memories of the most distant times. My own feeling, and of course it is nothing more than an opinion, is that we transcend death, not as individual memory-systems, but only in so far as our true identity is the total process of the world as distinct from the apparently separate organism.

As I have said, this sense of being the whole process is frequently experienced with LSD, and, for me, it has often arisen out of a strong feeling of the mutuality of opposites. Line and plane, concept and percept, solid and space, figure and ground, subject and object appear to be so completely correlative as to be convertible into each other. At one moment it seems that there are, for example, no lines in nature: there are only the boundaries of planes, boundaries which are, after all, the planes themselves. But at the next moment, looking carefully into the texture of these planes, one discovers them to be nothing but a dense network of patterned lines. Looking at the form of a tree against the sky, I have felt at one moment that its outline "belongs" to the tree, exploding into space. But the next moment I feel that the same form is the "inline" of the sky, of space imploding the tree. Every pull is felt as a push, and every push as a pull, as in rotating the rim of a wheel with one's hand. Is one pushing or pulling?

The sense that forms are also properties of the space in which they expand is not in the least fantastic when one considers the nature of magnetic fields, or, say, the dynamics of swirling ink dropped into water. The concepts of verbal thought are so clumsy that we tend to think only of one aspect of a relationship at a time. We alternate between seeing a given form as a property of the figure and as a property of the ground, as in the Gestalt image of two profiles in black silhouette, about to kiss. The white space between them appears as a chalice, but it is intensely difficult to see the kissing faces and the chalice simultaneously. Yet with LSD one appears to be able to feel this simultaneity quite vividly, and thus to become aware of the mutuality of one's own form and action and that of the surrounding world. The two seem to shape and determine each other at the same moment, explosion and implosion concurring in perfect harmony, so giving rise to the feeling that one's actual self is both. This inner identity is felt with every level of the environment—the physical world of stars and space, rocks and plants, the social world of human beings, and the ideational world of art and literature, music and conversation. All are grounds or fields operating in the most intimate mutuality with one's own existence and behavior so that the "origin" of action lies in both at once, fusing them into a single act. It is certainly for this reason that LSD taken in common with a small group can be a profoundly eucharistic experience, drawing the members together into an extremely warm and intimate bond of friendship.

All in all, I have felt that my experiments with this astonishing chemical have been most worth while, creative, stimulating, and, above all, an intimation that "there is more in heaven and earth than is dreamed of in your philosophy." Only once have I felt terror, the sense of being close to madness, and even here the insight gained was well worth the pain. Yet this was enough to convince me that indiscriminate use of this alchemy might be exceedingly dangerous, and to make me ask who, in our society, is competent to control its use. Obviously, this applies even more to such other powers of science as atomic energy, but once something is known there is really no way of locking it up. At the present time, 1960, LSD is in the control of pharmacologists and a few research groups of psychiatrists, and though there are unscrupulous and frankly psychotic psychiatrists, this seems to me a far more reliable form of control than that exercised by the police and the Bureau of Narcotics—which is not control at all, but ineffective repression, handing over actual control to the forces of organized crime.

On the whole, we feel justified in using dangerous powers when we can establish that there is a relatively low probability of disaster. Life organized so as to be completely foolproof and secure is simply not worth living, since it requires the final abolition of freedom. It is on this perfectly rational principle of gambling that we justify the use of travel by air and automobile, electric appliances in the home, and all the other dangerous instruments of civilization. Thus far, the record of catastrophes from the use of LSD is extremely low, and there is no evidence at all that it is either habit-forming or physically deleterious. It is, of course, possible to become psychically dependent on stimuli which do not establish any craving that can be identified in physiological terms. Personally, I am no example of phenomenal will power, but I find that I have no inclination to use LSD in the same way as tobacco or wines and liquors. On the contrary, the experience is always so fruitful that I feel I must digest it for some months before entering into it again. Furthermore, I find that I am quite instinctively disinclined to use it without the same sense of readiness and dedication with which one approaches a sacrament, and also that the experience is worth while to the precise degree that I keep my critical and intellectual faculties alert.

It is generally felt that there is a radical incompatibility between intuition and intellect, poetry and logic, spirituality and rationality. To me, the most impressive thing about LSD experiences is that these formally opposed realms seem instead to complement and fructify one another, suggesting, therefore, a mode of life in which man is no longer an embodied paradox of angel and animal, of reason fighting instinct, but a marvellous coincidence in whom Eros and Logos are one.

BIBLIOGRAPHY OF THE WORKS
OF ALAN W. WATTS

BOOKS:

1 *The Spirit of Zen.* John Murray, London, 1936. 2nd ed., 1955. 3rd ed., 1958. (Paper) Grove Press, New York, 1960.

(German) *Vom Geist des Zen.* Benno Schwabe, Basel and Stuttgart, 1956.

(Italian) *Lo Zen.* Bompiani, Milan, 1959.

2 *The Legacy of Asia and Western Man.* John Murray, London, 1937. University of Chicago, 1939.

(Dutch) *Azië en het Avondland.* Kluwer, Deventer, 1938.

3 *The Meaning of Happiness.* Harper, New York, 1940. 2nd ed., Delkin, Stanford, 1953.

4 *Behold the Spirit.* Pantheon, New York, 1947. Murray, London, 1948.

5 *Easter—Its Story and Meaning.* Henry Schuman (Abelard-Schuman), New York, 1950.

6 *The Supreme Identity.* Pantheon, New York, and Faber & Faber, London, 1950. (Paper) Noonday, New York, 1958.

7 *The Wisdom of Insecurity.* Pantheon, New York, 1951. Rider, London, 1952.

(German) *Weisheit des Ungesicherten Lebens.* Otto-Wilhelm-Barth, Munich, 1955.

8 *Myth and Ritual in Christianity.* Thames & Hudson, London, and Vanguard, New York, 1953. (Paper) Grove Press, New York, 1960.

(German) *Mythos und Ritus im Christentum.* Otto-Wilhelm-Barth, Munich, 1956.

9 *The Way of Zen.* Pantheon, New York, and Thames & Hudson, London, 1957. (Paper) Mentor Books, New York, 1959.

10 *Nature, Man, and Woman.* Pantheon, New York, and Thames & Hudson, London, 1958. (Paper) Mentor Books, New York, 1960.

MONOGRAPHS & PAMPHLETS:

11 *An Outline of Zen Buddhism.* Golden Vista Press, London, 1932.

12 *Seven Symbols of Life.* Buddhist Society, London, 1936.

13 *The Psychology of Acceptance.* Analytical Psychology Club of New York, 1939.

14 *The Theologia Mystica of St. Dionysius.* Trs. from the Greek with an introduction. Holy Cross Press, West Park, New York, 1944.

15 *The Meaning of Priesthood.* Advent Papers, Boston, 1946.

16 *Zen Buddhism.* The Buddhist Society, London, 1947.

(Dutch) *Zen Buddhisme.* H. Buys, Lochem, 1949.

17 *Zen.* (Expanded version of 16.) Delkin, Stanford, 1948.

18 *The Way of Liberation in Zen Buddhism.* American Academy of Asian Studies, San Francisco, 1955.

19 *Beat Zen, Square Zen, and Zen.* (Expanded version of 28.) City Lights Books, San Francisco, 1959.

MAJOR ARTICLES:

20 "The Rusty Swords of Japan." *Asia*, May, 1939. New York.

21 "How Buddhism Came to Life." *Asia*, October, 1939. New York.

22 "The Problem of Faith and Works in Buddhism." *Review of Religion*, vol. 5, 4; May, 1941. Columbia Univ., New York.

23 "The Negative Way." *Vedanta and the West*, vol. 14, 4; 1951. Hollywood. Also in *Vedanta for Modern Man*, ed. Christopher Isherwood. Harper, New York, 1951.

24 "Asian Psychology and Modern Psychiatry." *American Journal of Psychoanalysis*, vol. 13, 1, 1953. New York. Also in *Psychopathology*, ed. Reed, Alexander, and Tomkins. Harvard, Cambridge, 1958.

25 "The Language of Metaphysical Experience." *Journal of Religious Thought*, vol. 10, 2, 1953. Howard Univ., Washington, D.C.

26 "Oriental 'Omnipotence.'" *Tomorrow*, vol. 4, 1, 1955. New York.

27 "Convention, Conflict, and Liberation." *American Journal of Psychoanalysis*, vol. 16, 63, 1956.

28 "Beat Zen, Square Zen, and Zen." *Chicago Review*, vol. 12, 2, 1958.

29 "Zen and the Problem of Control." *Contact*, vol. 1, 1, 1958. Sausalito, Calif.

ARTICLES BY OTHERS:

30 Philip Wheelwright, "The Philosophy of Alan W. Watts." *Sewanee Review*, vol. 61, 3, 1953.

ALAN WATTS, who held both a master's degree in theology and a doctorate of divinity, has earned the reputation of being one of the most original and "un-rutted" philosophers of the century. He was best known as an interpreter of Zen Buddhism in particular, and of Indian and Chinese philosophy in general. He is the author of more than twenty books on the philosophy and psychology of religion, including (in Vintage Books) *Behold the Spirit; The Book; Does It Matter; The Joyous Cosmology; Nature, Man and Woman; The Supreme Identity; The Way of Zen; The Wisdom of Insecurity; Beyond Theology;* and *Cloud Hidden, Whereabouts Unknown.* He died in 1973.